IT'S
NOT
FAIR!

IT'S NOT FAIR!

Parenting Your Bright and Challenging Child

GILL HINES and ALISON BAVERSTOCK

piatkus

PIATKUS

First published in Great Britain in 2009 by Piatkus
Reprinted 2009

A CIP catalogue record for this book is available from the British Library

ISBN 978-0-7499-4046-1

Typeset in Sabon by M Rules
Printed and bound in Great Britain by MPG Books, Bodmin, Cornwall

Papers used by Piatkus are natural, renewable and
recyclable products sourced from well-managed forests and certified in
accordance with the rules of the Forest Stewardship Council.

Mixed Sources
Product group from well-managed
forests and other controlled sources
www.fsc.org Cert no. SGS-COC-004081
© 1996 Forest Stewardship Council
FSC

Piatkus
An imprint of
Little, Brown Book Group
100 Victoria Embankment
London EC4Y 0DY

An Hachette UK Company
www.hachette.co.uk

www.piatkus.co.uk

Acknowledgements

We would like to thank the following:

Elaine England, Head Teacher at Sheen Mount Primary School in Richmond and Mandy Morris, Inclusions Manager; the head teachers, staff and pupils at Merton Park Primary School, Merton, and Malden Parochial Primary School, Kingston, and numerous friends and colleagues who have helped, but did not wish to be acknowledged by name. The extracts from the work of Kirsty Gunn and Judy Blume are reproduced with kind permission. Finally we thank our publishers, our agent Jenny Brown and our partners, families and friends.

Contents

Foreword by Dame Jacqueline Wilson

I seem to specialise in writing about bright and challenging children. I chuckled at the definition of such children in this calm and comforting book: 'a bright and challenging child is smart, sassy and sparky mixed with just a hint of precociousness. At best they have an unshakeable self-belief – at worst a touch of arrogance.' Well, that's Tracy Beaker summed up in a nutshell. It's great fun writing about a child as bratty and bumptious as my fictional Tracy, but it's much harder dealing with a real bright and challenging child, on the go and showing off from the moment they bounce out of bed. Though they have many lovable traits and may grow into interesting and high-achieving talented adults, they can be a total pain to their siblings and a source of enormous anxiety and frustration to their parents. Teachers too find it a real strain coping with such children who are determined to dominate in the classroom.

It's easy enough for older, traditional adults to mutter, 'What that child needs is a good slapping.' We've moved on from the sparing the rod, spoiling the child days – and besides, conventional old-fashioned punishment is seldom if ever effective when it comes to bright attention-seeking children. However, we need to give our children sensible guidance as well as unconditional love. We need to set firm boundaries – and stick to them!

Gill Hines and Alison Baverstock have written a wise

and compassionate guidebook to parenting, with many practical suggestions. Their understanding and sensible advice should help us learn how to deal happily and successfully with *all* children, not just those who are bright and challenging.

Introduction

Does the world really need a book on how to parent bright and challenging children? After all, surely 'bright' and 'challenging' are the two things we want our children to be: sparky enough to take advantage of all the opportunities life throws at them, and not willing to be put off course by someone telling them that what they want is not possible, for a variety of reasons – or maybe for no reason at all, other than that they were not able to do it 'when I was your age'.

Most parents bring to the raising of their own families the issues that bothered them when they were children themselves. So if you were told as a child that 'because I said so' was a good enough reason for not doing something, you may want your own children to think for themselves, not just take what others say at face value.

A few years down the line, however, you may find you have children who have adopted this principle a little too strongly for your liking, who argue the toss about everything, engage with adults on an equal basis and – you fear – are inconsiderate and intolerant members of society. And, what is more, you may suspect that they are not themselves particularly happy.

That's where this book comes in. We take the positive traits, of which bright and challenging children have so many, and look at how to develop them in context – within their relationship with you, their family and wider society – so that they develop into well-adjusted, responsible and thoughtful adults. It is our hope that happier and more fulfilling relationships will result, for everyone.

Who this book is for

This book is for the parents, carers and teachers of children aged eight to twelve.

Parents are always asking us for help and support with their teenagers. The problems are fairly predictable – staying out late, communication, bad language and so on – and while we can offer advice and suggestions, the truth is that it is often too late to change things entirely; it becomes a matter of managing rather than undoing the situation.

Parenting teenagers begins at the age of eight. That is when they are no longer small children who think their parents and teachers are infallible and know all there is to know about life. It is also about the age at which children start to develop their own private and individual life. We're not suggesting that their personality, behaviour, tastes and character traits are fully formed at this age, but their independence from the adults around them in terms of both thought and action is growing daily.

Parents and educators alike share a common goal in seeking to help children to become self-actualised and well-socialised adults. This book is about that 'in-between' time, when they are no longer small children who can be moulded, nor yet set in patterns of behaviour that might challenge the status quo in the family.

Anyone with experience of teenagers knows that many of those who are exceptional in some way find life harder than their peers. This book is about helping these children to develop as independent young people who are not going to find themselves ostracised, victimised or disliked by those around them (with all the inherent dangers that such social isolation can lead to), while still retaining their special spark. This book is also for anyone who has contact with this age group, whether living with them, supporting or working with them. As an example of this in practice, Gill recently ran a workshop in which a grandmother and a foster carer took part, and which both found very helpful. In short, anyone who spends time with a child or children aged eight to twelve will find this book useful.

Who we are and why we've written this book

Gill Hines

This book is based on the workshops I run in schools; the original workshop was run at the request of Elaine England (Head Teacher at Sheen Mount Primary School in Richmond), who, as an educator, was becoming increasingly concerned about the number of headstrong children coming through the school and with the many parents who sought her out to ask advice. It was Elaine who coined the phrase 'bright and challenging' and set the wheels in motion.

For many years I have run successful workshops for parents, young people and children, as well as for the professionals who work with them. As a respected trainer, I have worked with diverse groups in the UK and in Europe, but my area of specialism remains parents and children.

My workshops are offered usually in schools. They are organised by school staff, local-authority representatives or parent associations and are generally offered free of charge to participants. The workshops follow similar formats and provide parents with the opportunity to explore issues with other parents in a friendly and fun way. Some of the exercises I use in the workshops and some of the handouts I give to parents are included in this book. Most workshops have a maximum of thirty participants and a minimum of six, so they are small enough to enable everyone to feel comfortable, but big enough for participants to remain anonymous should they wish to be so.

Among the hugely enthusiastic reviews posted on Amazon for our last book, *Whatever! A Down-to-earth Guide to Parenting Teenagers*, was a comment that it was unacceptable for someone who was not a parent to teach classes in parenting. We agree. There is a world of difference between telling other people how to parent their children and giving parents a forum in which to explore and discuss parenting issues together, and that is what I do so successfully.

In an average week I run between two and five workshops, and over the last ten years over 98 per cent of participants have graded them 'Good' or 'Excellent'.

When approached by Elaine, I jumped at the chance to work with a group of parents on the topic, and the first Bright and Challenging Child programme was run over six weeks in partnership with Mandy Morris, the Inclusions Manager at the school. This has been modified and repeated several times since, in a range of different venues and settings.

This book has grown out of my work with parents who have taken part in the programme and I'm delighted to share what I have learnt here in this book.

Alison Baverstock

I am a former publisher who now writes and teaches at Kingston University. I write mostly about writing and how to get published, although I have also written widely for the national press on a variety of issues. A mother of four, I first met Gill through attending some of her workshops, and was immediately impressed by her down-to-earth common sense (which I came to see, is not that common). We first formed a writing partnership to produce *Whatever! A Down-to-earth Guide to Parenting Teenagers* (published in 2005 and reprinted many times since) and I was delighted to be asked to work with her again on this new project.

For me the process has been both enlightening and uplifting. I have come to realise that there is an element of the 'bright and challenging' in all of us, and thinking about how we manage that – and could perhaps have managed it better in the past – has been at times a painful process. Along the way I have explored many new techniques, had renewed confidence to put others into practice, and seen measurable benefits result.

The bottom line is that we are all acutely aware of the selfish acts of others as they impact on us – from the person on their mobile phone on the early morning train, having a loud conversation when everyone else is half asleep, to the driver who cuts you up on the motorway. But if, in addition to spotting what irritates us as adults, we are attuned to identifying similar behaviour in both ourselves and our children – and try to think about how it both impacts on others and could be better managed in future – we are likely to live in a world that works better for all.

Is giving a child a label really going to help?

Children are individuals with distinct and complex person-
alities and many people may feel that applying a label is
unhelpful. We are certainly not suggesting we call bright and
challenging children that to their face – or even to other parents. It is not a widely used term, but simply an easy way to
describe a set of traits or behaviours which you may be able
to recognise and identify in your children and which we, and
many others, believe is on the increase.

How to use this book

The feedback from our first book *Whatever!* has told us that
readers appreciated its interactive nature, and that they
enjoyed being able to dip into it for guidance on a particular
issue, then return for a more in-depth read later.

With this in mind, we have again included a question and
answer section in each chapter for quick reference, as well as
top tips for some of the simple-to-use techniques that can be
really helpful on a day-to-day basis. 'Chapter snapshots'
provide an overview of what is to follow within each chapter. You'll also find some 'reflection exercises' to help you
challenge any negative thoughts or creeping doubts you have
about yourself as a parent.

Overall, we aim to support and encourage you to help
your children be happier and safer as they grow.

Gill Hines and Alison Baverstock
March 2009

1

THE BASICS

What Is a 'Bright and Challenging Child'?

CHAPTER SNAPSHOT

This chapter will help you to understand what we mean by the term 'bright and challenging child' (or B&C child for short) and the typical behavioural and personality traits that this might encompass. It will also make it easier for you to recognise some of the reasons why your child might develop these traits, so you can work with them where needed in order to channel their energies in a more positive direction. This way they won't face additional difficulties as they approach their teenage years. This chapter will also give you an idea of the issues that the book as a whole is discussing, as well as the tools you will need to identify those which are of importance to you and your child.

Spotting the 'bright and challenging' child

A bright and challenging child is smart, sassy and sparky, with just a hint of precociousness. At best, they have an unshakeable self-belief; at worst, a touch of arrogance.

While they do have many positive qualities, and will

probably be very successful in their chosen paths in life, bright and challenging children can be both difficult to parent and exhausting to teach, due to their confident belief that they are cleverer and more capable than the rest of us. And although this is, in some cases, undoubtedly true, they are at risk because – as much as they don't want to admit it – they don't understand the world we live in, the nuances of human nature or the dangers of modern life anywhere near as well as we older and wiser folk do.

It is for this very reason that these children can be hard to parent. You know best about many things, but your child won't accept guidance, advice or restrictions from you, unless you can prove them wrong. And, as they are hardly ever wrong in their own eyes, this is an arduous task and an endless, thankless battle.

No wonder then that many parents of B&C children eventually let them go their own way with fingers crossed and fear in their hearts, far sooner than less headstrong siblings would be encouraged to do. This may mean that they lose their way or even enter into risky behaviours as they go all out to prove that they are the pack leaders who push back the boundaries from a young age. It is not uncommon to hear of such children going all-night clubbing as young as thirteen or fourteen, or taking an unsupervised holiday with friends at fourteen or fifteen. They often choose to be with older young people too, so may be more likely than others to get into age-inappropriate activities before their peers. All of this makes the B&C child remarkably vulnerable to exploitation and abuse as well as exposing them to many of the pitfalls of modern-day youth, only without the skills or maturity needed to handle them.

Recognising the bright and challenging child

While all children are, of course, different, there are many traits and behaviours which, if appearing all together or to a pronounced degree, might lead you to identify a child as bright and challenging. If you find that your child often outsmarts you or you frequently just don't know how to deal with a particular situation because they manage to 'wrong-foot' you, we would say you probably have a B&C child on your hands. Essentially, we believe that it's a 'gut feeing' – if it seems to fit, the chances are it does – but here are some of the characteristics to look out for:

1. They are verbally able

The B&C child can usually express him or herself very well. They are able to verbalise tricky concepts and ideas and may use words and wordplay to try and trip up the rest of the world. They may even try and 'score points' with their clever linguistic skills, twisting meaning in everyday conversation.

Example
When asked (for the third time) to tidy her room, eight-year-old Martha replies: 'Only last week you were telling me to get more exercise and fresh air – now when I want to do as I'm told you go and tell me to go indoors and tidy my room.'

2. They won't accept boundaries as fixed

They demand the right to negotiate everything – every time. So routines such as bedtime or mealtimes become everyday battles, as they try to get the rules changed to suit their needs.

Example

Nine-year-old Luke at his set bedtime says, 'I'm not tired at all, and if I go to bed now I won't sleep and I won't get tired either because I'm not using any energy – my brain will just go whirr, whirr. If I just play this a bit more then I'll be much more tired and in the end I'll sleep more anyway.'

3. They have to win

No matter what they are doing the B&C child just has to win at it. They have to prove that they are cleverer, faster, clearer-thinking and all-round superior to everyone else. This can be particularly tiresome if you have more than one such child in the family (or, heaven help you, a B&C partner!).

Furthermore, a B&C child may simply not co-operate or participate if they don't feel they can win. Younger children may well sulk or throw a tantrum every time something comes along that means they will not be able to shine.

Example

Eight-year-old Rufus is at a family party where children aged three to twelve are present. He refuses to join in the running races and will only participate in the four-a-side football game if the two oldest boys are in his team.

4. Keen to challenge

The B&C child never takes what you say at face value. They want proof. It is not uncommon to hear them say something like, 'How do you know that?' when presented with a fact, particularly if that fact is being used to back up something you are asking them to do. They will also challenge your authority to ask them to do whatever it is in the first place.

This may be particularly obvious when there is a step-parent involved whose authority is constantly questioned.

Example

At the dinner table, ten-year-old Carlotta is told to eat her broccoli because it's good for her. 'How do you know it's good for me?' she asks. 'I mean, for all you know, I have a hidden broccoli allergy and one day I might die from it. And anyway, it's not fair you telling me what to eat because you don't let me tell you what to eat.'

5. Easily bored

The B&C child's sharp mind likes to be stimulated at all times. This means they can easily become bored and expect as a right that you will give them your undivided attention and help them to find something to do. A bored child can easily become a catalyst for sibling rows and fights too, all of which will be your fault for not having helped them to get un-bored.

Some children can seem quite rude when their attention lapses mid-conversation, and adults from outside the immediate circle may be quite judgemental of the child who switches off or states, simply, 'I'm bored', in a loud voice while the adult is talking. (Ask any teacher!)

Example

Eight-year-old Shapla has been happily reading in her room all morning. She has been deaf to all attempts to engage her in any activity, including an outing to the park on her bike or a trip to town shopping, with the promise of lunch in a café. 'I'm bored,' she says. 'Why is it so boring in this family? We never do anything fun. I wish it was a school day. School is boring but not as boring as home.'

6. They know which of your buttons to push for maximum impact

The B&C child seems to know instinctively how to get you in their power. Whether it's pushing your guilt button, your anger button, your sympathy button or your embarrassment button, they can do it in one blow. Because they are clever and verbally able it is easy for them. They have watched you and unconsciously worked out your weaknesses. They will do whatever they need to get their own way, with few qualms about doing so, however much you squirm.

Example
Eight-year-old Edward has just been told that he can't go and play at a friend's house today as Mum is too busy to take him. 'Too busy? You're always too busy. I don't know why you had me if you are so busy. You had time to talk to Anna on the phone this morning and to go shopping. You're only too busy to do what I want.'

You should now have a better idea of whether or not your child fits the bright and challenging mould. If, however, you still need more help deciding, take the time to complete the short questionnaire at the end of this chapter.

Pros and cons of the bright and challenging child

It's not all bad, and there are many positive aspects to the B&C child.

- They think for themselves
- They are often very funny and good company
- They give you lots to think about and plenty to talk about

- They can be very stimulating
- Keeping up with them can help you to develop new skills and learn new things
- There are lots of times when they make you proud
- They keep you on your toes – and while they may not stop you getting old, they certainly keep you active and involved
- They are interested – they want to learn, though not always about the things you think they should!

However, there are also many difficulties to overcome when parenting the B&C child:

- Explanations are always required, as well as constant reaffirmation of boundaries
- Dealing with them is so tiring, because you are never finished, the boxes are never all ticked
- They can be superior and tend towards arrogance
- Their constant questioning can be undermining
- They are not restful – literally, because they don't sleep much, but also, they are not relaxing company
- You worry about them: they may have trouble interacting socially with peers, or their general wilfulness and inclination towards risk can be a concern
- They are inclined to be sarcastic, which can be catching within a family
- Their immense confidence can be worrying when you see what is coming, but they don't
- They are not good at *not* succeeding and can be quite thrown by (and turn nasty on) failure
- They take up a lot of attention, which can be hard on other children and partners, as well as yourself

- They tend not to learn from mistakes – because they don't accept that they have made any. This leaves them inclined to blame others, which can cause problems and arguments
- The family can seem more harmonious without them around; this in turn sometimes leads to feelings of guilt

The bright and challenging child – a new phenomenon?

Many parents want to know if bright and challenging children are born or grow that way – in other words, is it nature or nurture that makes them what they are? The simple answer is that these children have been around for ever, but perhaps in past generations they would have had some of their personality traits rigorously suppressed. Modern parenting styles, on the other hand, have supported a growth in numbers of the children who fit our profile: today's parents tend to be more permissive, encouraging a child's personality to flourish, sometimes at the cost of important elements of socialisation. So there is a combination of factors at work:

> Intelligence + Personality + Parenting
> = Bright and Challenging Children

Of course, there are many variables within each of these 'components', but there does seem to be a specific mixture of traits which, when added together, makes a child what they are.

Firstly, these children are naturally bright. Whether they do well at school academically is neither here nor there; it is their quick minds and ability to read people and situations succinctly that makes them 'bright' in this context.

We've already looked at some of the features of the bright and challenging child, but let's now consider the parenting methods most commonly associated with them:

- Encouraging negotiation at an early age by giving complex reasons why things should, or should not be done. This leads the child to understand that if they can break down the argument, they can change the 'rules' (and too often they can)
- Weak or shifting boundaries – saying 'No', then giving in to their questions or arguments
- Overcompensating – giving in to a child's demands or trying too hard to please them due to guilt or insecurity about your parenting or the time you have to give them
- Wanting to be seen as 'fair' or as a 'best friend', which can make it difficult to say 'No'
- Misreading their facility with language and believing that they are wiser than they are
- Encouraging children to argue and be more assertive
- Confusing intelligence with maturity
- Being tired and apathetic – this is particularly applicable if the B&C child is born later on in the family

This book will help you to identify ways in which changing your parenting could help your child change their behaviour. We certainly don't want to alter their personality or their intelligence – both are to be cherished and encouraged – but by reining them in while they are young enough for you to do so, you may prevent a lot of problems and potential dangers in the future.

Quiz: identifying the bright and challenging child

You may have already made your decision based on what you've read so far, but, if you are still unsure, this quick quiz may help you make your mind up.

	Usually or always	Some- times	Not often or never
1. When asked to do something they don't want to do, they give logical and reasoned arguments for why they should not be asked to do it.			
2. When playing with other children they are very bad losers.			
3. They know how to make you feel guilty and they do so when it suits them.			
4. They refuse to participate in things they will not be able to shine at.			
5. They are unkind or boastful with less able/younger siblings or friends.			
6. They make observations and comments that seem very sophisticated for their years.			
7. They can be great fun to be with and have a sharp and keen observational humour.			
8. When having one-to-one time with you they seem to change completely and are compliant, friendly, cheerful and good company.			
9. There are areas, hobbies or interests at which they excel.			
10. They don't accept your right to tell them what to do.			

Scoring
Score 1 point for each time you have answered 'Not often or never'.
Score 2 points for each time you have answered 'Sometimes'.
Score 3 points for each time you have answered 'Usually or always'.

0–15 points
They are probably challenging at times in the way that all children can be and you'll know yourself or from school if they are bright but they are probably not the child we are calling 'bright and challenging' in this book. You may still find plenty of useful ideas and tips here to help you parent.

15–23 points
Well, they are certainly what we call 'bright and challenging'. The good news is that they are either still quite young or you have developed good coping strategies already – or both. We think we still have plenty to offer in terms of supporting you as your child grows with ideas, techniques and reassurance.

23–30 points
You really didn't need to do the quiz did you? Of course you have a bright and challenging child. In fact, your life is probably dominated by them when you are together. This book will help, reassure, prompt and guide you through new ways of parenting them that might make both you and your child more content as they grow into their teens.

So, where do you begin?

Well, the first thing to do is to recognise whether you have a bright and challenging child or not.

Next, accept that parenting them is going to be hard work at times and an ongoing process, but it is also going to be a tremendous learning experience, a source of great joy, entertainment and pleasure too. All parents feel proud of their children, but when you realise how far they have come and that you have helped them to make those steps one by one, you are also allowed to be a little proud of yourself.

You have to remember your child's need to win at all times, which will also mean accepting that rows and name-calling may follow any attempt to change their power tactics. Also, that they have a short route to what upsets you, and will push whichever button is necessary to achieve what they want. It's important to remember that regardless of how upset they – and you – may get, saying 'No' is not going to harm them. Rather, it is a way to slow down their headlong rush into the worst kind of independence – the kind that takes no notice of anyone else and lacks the requisite life skills to do well.

There is a world of difference between just being a parent and actively parenting. Good parenting is hard work and takes time. It comes without pay, the end results are not apparent for years and there is some recognition but not much, so although you may get thanked one day, we wouldn't bank on it.

This may be tough to read, but it sums up why so many people choose the easy option of peace and harmony over doing what will help their children become well-rounded adults. No doubt there will be times when it all seems too difficult, but there will be others when seeing the changes in them will give you enough of a boost to keep going.

Positive feedback from others is also a great reward, so don't be afraid to ask for some. Partners, teachers, siblings and friends will all notice the changes as they happen.

Through it all, you'll probably have to work on your own self-esteem at times, so you don't feel threatened by the challenges ahead or dragged down by the effort of change. You will need to believe that it's worth the struggle when things are tough and to keep reminding yourself that letting your child have their own way all the time is actually harmful to them – even if in the short term it brings peace and calm.

Questions and answers

Q. *My ten-year-old son is streets ahead of his classmates in almost all his schoolwork; he is able to make sensible decisions and choices about how he spends his time and we almost never have to talk to him about his behaviour. He tends to stay up on the computer late at night but we consider this to be his prerogative, as it certainly isn't affecting his performance at school. He doesn't take much notice of his younger sister, so doesn't argue much with her. In fact, he's no problem at all as long as he's treated in a mature and adult fashion. Why on earth should I try and change him?*
A. No one is saying you should. If you're all happy with the status quo then you are very fortunate indeed and we wish you well. Many parents would envy you as they pick up yet another wet towel from the bathroom floor or follow the trail of dirty football kit all over the house. My only concern would be on the nature and purpose of childhood and whether your son is actually having the childhood that will help him become a well-rounded adult.

You say nothing of friends and play, nothing of fun and mischief, nothing of learning to explore and manage emotions. All of these things have their place in a child's life, and, in our opinion, without them the child is missing out on some of the key experiences needed to learn and grow.

Have a look at the quiz on page 16 and answer it

honestly. Then maybe you can answer your question for yourself one way or the other.

Q. *My eight-year-old daughter is a nightmare. She rules over the house like a queen and tells everyone what to do and how to do it. She throws real temper tantrums like a three-year-old when she doesn't get her own way about even the smallest thing, like what to watch on the TV, and she has everyone tiptoeing around her. The school say she's pretty much the same there too, although she's clever and gets on with her work well. She is fine when everything goes her way, and she can be the life and soul of the family – our little Princess. We love her to bits, but I worry that she's going to get totally out of control when she gets older. We've tried to talk to her about her behaviour but she says she understands, then behaves in exactly the same way next time. What can we do to get her to see that she can't have her own way all the time?*

A. Your daughter sounds like the classic bright and challenging child – particularly as she is still only eight years old! You are right to be concerned for the future – she has the potential to become a very difficult and unlikeable teenager and life might become quite hard for her in later life unless she changes.

However, it's not just her that has to change. It's you as well. She is simply reacting to the way in which she has been raised and will continue to do so, unless something shifts radically. You must stop calling her 'Princess', for a start – it usually means a girl who gets away with murder, and she has to stop getting away with quite a lot of things.

You need to spell out for her what she can and can't do, and make sure she is rewarded with lots of attention and smiles when she gets it right, as well as being given clear sanctions and the withdrawal of attention and smiles when she chooses to behave badly. She has to learn through consistent approval/disapproval, backed up by exclusion from the family unit when she fails to show respect for it by breaking the accepted code of behaviour. You'll find much to help you in this book and her school should be able to help too, if you ask them for their support. Change can be painful and it might require some serious soul-searching on your part to look at why you have parented your daughter in the way that you have and how it feels when you do it differently and upset her.

But just remember that in the end she will be a better, more socialised and more likeable person for it all. If you learn to put your foot down, show her your feelings – not just 'reason' – and let her take some responsibility for her behaviour and its impact, things will change quite dramatically.

2
GOOD DAYS AND BAD
Conflict and Harmony

CHAPTER SNAPSHOT

This chapter is about your relationship with your child. We will be exploring the way you look at and talk about your child's behaviour. Rather than being amazed, flabbergasted, enraged or amused by what they do, you will need to ask yourself some searching questions to get to the root of the behaviour and the many pathways through time where your child's emerging traits have been reinforced or strengthened, albeit unconsciously.

By learning to spot patterns in their behaviour, you will begin to identify the changes that should be made in order to alter the path for the future. A word of warning though before we start: this might not be easy, and may mean that you end up changing the way you have always done things. This will require honesty on your part and will probably not feel comfortable.

The make-up of the bright and challenging child

As we've already seen in Chapter 1, there are three key factors at play in the bright and challenging child: intelligence, personality and parenting. This does not mean that anyone is to blame for your child being the way they are: most parents of B&C children are everything a child could wish for, and many have other children who are well behaved and responsive. But neither is the child's behaviour solely down to them or their genetics. The problem arises when you have a mixture of three main elements:

- A very intelligent individual who thinks fast and can reason quickly – usually with very well-developed verbal ability
- A child with a personality that craves (more than most) to be the centre of attention at all times; they love to be in the spotlight
- A child who has been allowed to negotiate everything from an early age and sees nothing as fixed – it can all be changed if they can come up with the right ploy!

How gender impacts on treatment of B&C children

As an identifier, 'bright and challenging' is not gender-specific, but in our work with parents we have come across far more sons than daughters being identified in this way, and seen as difficult. We don't believe that there is any difference between the intelligence of girls and boys, nor do we believe that fewer girls than boys have the personality traits associated with the B&C child. If anything, more girls than boys seem to be attention-seeking to a high degree and crave life in the spotlight. You only have to see the number of eight-year-old girls who want to be pop stars to realise that shrinking violets are a rare breed these days. So the fact that fewer girls are identified as B&C would seem to be down to the third ingredient in the mixture: parenting.

There was a time when boys were seen as more valuable

and intelligent than girls. But while society at large has moved on in terms of gender differences and value, we still haven't overcome the pervasive elements of gender stereotyping that still exist – some real and some assumed – and that might just tip the balance.

In terms of the B&C child, the qualities that are (often unwittingly) encouraged are:

- **Being verbally precocious,** cheeky or even quite rude – this is generally tolerated more in little boys than girls, who are expected to be polite and helpful
- **Not doing as they are told** – it is, perhaps, accepted that 'boys will be boys'; we believe that girls are worse tantrum-throwers than boys when they are small, yet more boys seem to be appeased while more girls are effectively managed

Perhaps this should not surprise us. Most care for small children comes from mothers and female carers who perhaps expect boys to be babyish and less able to control themselves; while girls are expected to be capable and multi-faceted like themselves. Many women openly infantilise their partners and men in general, both privately and publicly, so it's no wonder they may also tend to do the same to their male children.

Most parents feel that girls are more responsible for their actions because girls 'mature faster' than boys. This is used as an excuse for everything from weaning sooner, potty training earlier and expecting them to tidy up their rooms at a younger age. It is true, very generally speaking, that there are some differences in terms of maturation at certain stages of a child's development, but this is certainly not on the scale that some parents perceive it to be. You would be hardpressed to find a thirty-year-old woman who still gets her laundry done by her mother, but you will find plenty of men of the same age who do.

How position in the family impacts on treatment of B&C children

In our experience, the two most common B&C children are the only child and the youngest child. This is simply born of observation, and is in no way a scientific fact. However, while we have come across B&C children who are the eldest or middle child, and even a family of six such children, the tendency still persists that in a family where there are several children, and one who is B&C, it will be the youngest.

The only child

B&C only children are fairly easily explained. They have often been exposed mostly to adult company, received a lot of attention and have been encouraged to speak back in an adult manner from an early age. Without siblings to rub up against on a daily basis, they have had much less opportunity to be 'childish'. The adults looking after them have often taken the trouble to explain decision making, or the way of the world as they see it, in minute detail, and they have been taught to reason (as far as they are able). With no other siblings to compete with for attention, their boundaries have not needed to be reinforced, and they have often been allowed to make a lot of choices for themselves from an early age. Because they are intelligent and can speak and reason like little adults, they are often thought of as being more mature than they really are and provide hours of entertainment to everyone around them.

But whereas they are endlessly entertaining when they are four or five and still have cuteness on their side, as they grow older the precociousness and argumentativeness that were a part of their appeal start to grate and can begin to make them very unpopular with teachers and peers.

The youngest child

The younger child with B&C traits may have reached this point via two different routes.

The first is the relative isolation of the youngest child, who is marooned in their birth position, feeling that they will never to be as good at things as the rest of the family they join – that they are slowest to run in the family race, least likely to get things right on the TV quiz programme or too young to remember a key piece of family folklore. They may get teased or laughed at on a regular basis, and this can lead them to try to win at things they are good at; perhaps their verbal skills or quick wit. They learn to get attention and make everyone laugh with their jokes and puns, their candid observations or their charmingly simplistic views on everything. They become the centre of attention; the little star whose sayings are shared with family and friends with regular instalments of 'Guess what Johnny said yesterday?'

The other route is through relaxation of the family rules as the family gets bigger. Eldest children are often expected to shoulder some responsibility for younger siblings and to be paragons of virtue, as they can be seen as role models within the family. But rules are less strict by the time younger siblings come along, and the last to arrive often holds a special place in the hearts of parents and older siblings alike: everyone remembers their birth and can feel nostalgia for the baby who completed the family. They go on being petted for far longer than the older children, who had to accommodate a sibling and move on from being 'the baby'. This means they sometimes get away with things older siblings would be chastised for. On top of all this their parents are tired.

Having already worried themselves sick over number one's every cough and scratch and having had, perhaps, another one or two babies in between, they have let go of the reins quite a lot by the time this little star puts in an appearance. And so a B&C child is born.

Challenging assumptions

REFLECTION EXERCISE

Think back to the very first time you saw your bright and challenging child. Consider the very first ten minutes of their life – or the first ten minutes you can recall. How did they behave then that is just the same now? What element of their personality did they display that has never really changed?

_____

_____

_____

How did you respond to it then? _____
How did you feel about it then? _____

See if you can track that same personality trait when they were three or four years old.
How did you respond to it then? _____
How did you feel about it then? _____

Now reflect on how this same trait affects them and your relationship with them now.
How do you respond to it now? _____
How do you feel about it now? _____

This can be a powerful exercise. Did you manage to identify something in your child's personality now that has been recognisable from the very first moments of their life? Were they forceful, demanding, angry, content or curious – or all of the above?

Some of the features that parents have highlighted during this exercise are that their child was:

- bad-tempered
- curious
- laid-back
- angry
- sweet-natured
- grumpy
- feisty
- not bothered
- intelligent

Many parents also reported comments made by midwives, nurses or doctors; it seems common for those present at the birth of a child to make some kind of statement about the child's character or personality.

But what about the ways in which a particular trait or quality has developed and evolved throughout the child's life? Sometimes when you see something in a young child, or think you see it, you unconsciously reinforce that quality or trait – so that it grows and increases with time to meet your initial expectations. To some degree, your children become what you make them while they are young – so perhaps a little rewriting of your expectations may free a child to be a whole other person. Telling them they have always been kind, loving, generous, fair and even-tempered might just encourage them to live up to some new expectations with pride.

Of course, you can never be sure that the child who is seen as 'a complainer' at the moment of birth wouldn't have ended up being one in later life, but there is the possibility that they may be living up to the parental belief in the behaviour as what is expected.

As Gill recalls: 'I was always told that I was a miserable baby and whenever I was upset as a child my mother would remind me that I had been miserable from the moment of birth – the implication being that I was an incorrigible misery, and always would be. But I'm fairly sure that anyone who knows me now would not describe me that way; rather as optimistic and positive, albeit with a moody streak. Have I actually changed or have I simply stopped being judged by an out-of-date and possibly incorrect assumption?'

Example

The parents of Julia, a nine-year-old, remembered that the midwife who delivered her said – when she was less than half an hour old – that she 'has a temper on her and likes to get her own way'. Julia's parents recalled how they repeated this comment to relatives and friends countless times over the years and how Julia's behaviour had seemed to fit the midwife's early opinion.

Julia's parents, Aaron and Emma, could identify examples of how they had behaved differently with her from the way they were with their two sons. With Julia they tended to make much firmer statements; they expected her to 'make a fuss' and so tried to give her no leeway. With the boys they felt they needed much less emphasis as they were both more 'easy-going'.

After a little discussion, Aaron could see how the way in which he sometimes spoke to his daughter might actually be the reason why she felt frustrated and hard done by, especially in relation to how her brothers were treated. And while both parents still believed their daughter to have a worse temper than her brothers, they could also see not only how that belief had affected the way they dealt with her, but also that their hard-line approach might have contributed to the problems, in particular the difficulties Julia had with her siblings.

After just one week of adopting a more gentle approach, Emma reported that Julia had been in fewer arguments with her brothers and had had fewer confrontations with her father.

Recognising triggers

When Gill does workshops with parents, the very first thing she asks them to think about is the times when their child is a delight to be with. It's so easy to get hung up on how difficult parenting them can be, or how their immense self-confidence can render them so vulnerable. But mostly, these are great kids, and when conditions are right they bring great joy to everyone who knows them.

What creates harmony with a bright and challenging child?

Parents say that there is most likely to be harmony with their B&C child when:

- the child has their undivided attention
- it's one parent and one child
- they are doing what the child wants to do
- the child is being funny and everyone is laughing, so they are the life and soul of the party and the centre of attention

- the child is singled out for praise at school or by others and they are proud
- other people comment on something interesting or amusing that the child has done
- the child is demonstrating that he/she is good at something
- the child wants to know something and asks them to explain or do it with them
- everything is clear and ordered
- they are having an interesting or stimulating discussion with their child
- they are playing games or sports together with their child
- the child is doing new things
- the child has been praised
- the child is ill
- the child needs his/her parents

But perhaps the one overwhelming quality that always comes out is the child's sense of humour – so anything that allows that to shine will always work well.

What creates conflict with a B&C child?

Just as most parents can relate to the things that produce harmony with their child, there is a lot of common ground in the causes of conflict or disharmony, such as when:

- they are trying to change something in their child's behaviour
- there is something wrong or unacceptable in the child's behaviour and they want to correct them
- the child feels criticised by them or by their siblings – they won't give in and see the point (or even accept

that they have a point) but just keep changing the argument to try to attack back

- the child has had a bad day
- the child suddenly changes mood (often quite out of the blue) and becomes attacking
- the child feels he/she has been unfairly treated at school or by others; this upsets them and they bring it home
- if they have had a good time but do not feel everyone's attention is sufficiently focused on them
- there are issues of time management: when the child won't fit in with a wider picture or agreed boundaries, e.g. going to bed, getting up, even if it is for their own benefit (like getting to school on time) and they still resist
- the child is asked to tidy up or do other mundane domestic chores
- the child spots a weakness in someone else and can't resist showing it up
- the child is asked not to do something – and they feel they have an equal right to make all decisions and challenge them, even if the issue is one of basic safety or general benefit to the family as a whole

What can you do?

The first thing to do is to draw up your own list – on paper or in your head – of the things that cause harmony and the things that cause conflict in your home. Alternatively, tick the entries on the lists above that apply to you, and think hard if there are any others you could add. Whichever way you choose to compile your list, once it is complete, and you begin to see a pattern emerging, try to use the 'harmony' elements to diffuse the conflicts.

For example, if your child is being insufferably attention-seeking at the dinner table and keeps shouting everyone else down or belittling others' comments, rather than challenging them head-on, and asking them to stop because they are out of order, try the following:

1. Remember that the B&C child has a strong ego and hates to be put down in front of others. So if you challenge them head-on, as you would be perfectly justified in doing, they will simply turn up the volume on the existing behaviour, blame everyone else (and probably you in some way) for an unfair attack and, in the process, destroy any remaining family harmony and ruin everyone's meal. You don't want to be sitting at the table after everyone else has left in disgust.

2. Remember how they love to be dealt with one-to-one. Ask them to join you in another room, making a feasible excuse for this, such as helping you to get or find something because they are so good at getting or finding things, as applicable. A little flattery sometimes goes a long way.

3. Once the two of you are alone, suggest that they help you by changing their behaviour and that it's a secret between the two of you. It may sound a little devious and while we would not generally advocate being so manipulative, we also know that having one confrontation after another is not healthy for you or for other family members. (Sometimes it's worth bending the rules a little if it means a peaceful solution.) If they comply with your request, make sure you catch their eye and give them a wink, praise them, talk them up and generally give them your attention for behaving in all the right ways far more than you usually would.

Example

What *not* to do: eight-year-old Izzy has been holding forth about an episode of *The Simpsons* that she found very funny, while the rest of the family are watching something else on television. She keeps repeating a certain phrase over and over again, very loudly, and is getting on everyone's nerves. Dad suggests that they all ignore her, at which point Izzy gets up and starts to dance in front of the TV laughing loudly, daring the others to react. Mum, Dad and her two older brothers (aged ten and fourteen) are getting fed up and the eldest brother starts to harangue both Izzy and his mum for not telling her to shut up and sit down. An almighty row erupts with Izzy in tears and the brother storming out of the room in a temper.

The clever approach: instead of getting angry, Mum laughs and looks Izzy straight in the eye. 'What a wonderful dance Izzy,' she says. 'Come and give me a hug!' She holds on tight to Izzy and whispers in her ear. She whispers that they should have a game and invites Izzy to whisper in her ear so that no one else can hear. She then tells Izzy how well she is now behaving, how sensible she is being and how impressed she is that Izzy can be so quiet and sit so still when she tries. Izzy behaves really well as long as the reinforcement lasts.

Remember that the B&C child can't take criticism

The bright and challenging child responds badly to any attempt to point out their failings, however well meant or kindly phrased they are. So instead, you need to get them to recognise how their behaviour could be improved and praise them to the hilt for being clever enough to work it out.

Example

What *not* to do: ten-year-old Mac has been asked repeatedly to put his coat and bag away, but both are still lying on the floor, and each time he is asked he says, 'In a minute – I'm busy. I will do it, but in a minute.' Mum decides enough is enough and starts to shout at him. He mutters under his breath, then behaves badly all evening with lots of asides and 'attitude'.

The clever approach: Mum engages Mac's attention and makes eye contact. 'Sweetheart, I don't know what to do. I've got so many things to do and I can't decide which one to do next. I keep half starting something, then starting on something else. Can you spare me a minute to help me get myself sorted? I'd really appreciate it.'

As is the case with most B&C children, attention – in this case being singled out to perform an adult role and therefore assuming a level of superiority – wins Mac over and he not only clears away his bag and coat but tidies the living room (after a fashion) too.

Remember that the B&C child just has to win at all costs

No matter what situation they find themselves in, the bright and challenging child has to show they are top of the troupe. They will often not participate in things they cannot win at. But in everyday life, they make everything a contest: how fast they can eat their food; how quickly they can get dressed; how many times they can say a certain word without anyone noticing. Life is a competition to a B&C child.

Example

What *not* to do: nine-year-old Sean wants to go to a friend's house after tea to play but Mum has far too much on to take him and fetch him. She says she will arrange with the boy's mother to let him play tomorrow after school and they can go home together. But Sean is adamant that he wants to go today and gets really angry. First, he tries sulking and crossing his arms across his chest defiantly, but when this has no effect, he starts listing all his mother's failings. She juggles a part-time job and is already feeling guilty, so his accusation that 'she never has time for him' is a button with a direct line to her own conscience. At first, Mum gets upset at the things Sean says, but then she gets angry. A big shouting match ensues. Mum orders Sean to his room, but he refuses to go and starts throwing things around the house.

The clever approach: when Sean asks to go to his friend, Mum says, 'Of course you can, if you really want to. But you'll only get half an hour to play as it's quite late now. What a shame you didn't mention it earlier. We'd better ring David's mum to make sure she doesn't mind though. It's good actually, as I was going to suggest you went home with him straight from school tomorrow and stayed for tea – and so had more time with him. But if I take you now you can come straight home tomorrow as usual.'

Sean, of course, immediately sees the benefit of switching to tomorrow, both for himself and because he thought his mum preferred him to go today.

The downside of duplicity

By now you may well be feeling a little uncomfortable. If, like me, you are a pretty straightforward person, all of this may seem like a lot of effort and may well leave a slightly bad taste in your mouth. The truth is, you cannot change the behaviour of others, however hard you try. What you can change, however, is your own behaviour, and you can do so in such a way that others alter theirs in response to it. The bottom line is that it's your choice to keep the peace sometimes, rather than end up in a fight. And, of course, while all this is going on, you continue to work on the way the child behaves at other times; to concentrate on their core beliefs to help them change themselves. More of that later.

Everyday situations that cause conflict and suggestions for their harmonious resolution

1. When they have had a bad day at school

You need to encourage the bright and challenging child to let you know what has gone wrong, not just let them act it out when they get home. Give them the opportunity to offload. You could develop a system whereby they pass on the essentials of their day rather than being required to debrief you fully – few children want to relate everything that's happened the moment they get home, and the B&C child may be keen to work on a story ('spin') before sharing it. Simply asking, 'How was school today?' is a killer, because few children really know how to answer it.

So, how can you get the essential information – and help them get settled in for the evening, rather than encourage them to dwell on what went wrong? One quite simple method is to adopt a thumbs up/down/in the middle 'code' when you meet – a signal that you both employ to let the other know how the day has been. Conversation can then take place.

A simple chat on the way home is always good as it allows you both to get there with a clean slate. For example, getting your child to tell you something good, something bad and something mad or funny that happens every day will allow their creativity to develop. It will also mean they can let off steam if required, without dwelling too much on the things that upset them.

If you always dwell on the negatives of the day, you may be encouraging them to do the same – *during* the day. Make a point of being equally interested in all aspects of their stories. Non-controversial starting points, such as asking what was for lunch, can be effective.

Encourage them to separate parts of the day off from each other by having a ritual that forms a divide, for example by having a shower or kicking a football around (sometimes a good way of dealing with feelings).Try not to 'fix' their feelings for them by telling them to cheer up or giving them something you know they like to jolly them out of it. Let them have their feelings and work through them on their own, with support if they look for it.

2. When they feel they have been unfairly treated at school

Often, they may not have been, but just feel like they have. Someone else got what they wanted, or their pride was wounded, and to them this will always feel unfair.

If this is the case, it is very important for you as a parent to see the wider situation and not just blame the other pupils or the teacher, particularly in front of your child. Try to explain that unfairness can work both ways, and to encourage them to see the situation from both points of view. If you do give them the other perspective, however, they will probably accuse you of siding with the enemy, so try to tell a similar story involving different protagonists, or as something that has happened to you or a friend in the past or in a soap opera on television. Encourage them to explore *why* they think the unfair situation has arisen. Praise their intellectual engagement and thought processes while they do this to keep them going.

So, however tempting, try not to criticise or take sides, just explore what is going on. This will help your child be more objective. And remember that they will find it very difficult to say that they have done wrong, so concentrate instead on what they could do differently next time. If there is a real issue to discuss with a teacher, the fact that you have not been bombarding the school with complaints since the day your child started there will give more weight to your concerns when you do get in touch.

3. When they are having a good time

Laugh, share and encourage them to talk about others and not just themselves, but not in a critical way – change the subject if they are being spiteful or unkind (girls can be particularly prone to do this). Give them positive reinforcement when they are being funny, or telling positive stories about others. Help them to understand that discussing issues is a good thing; problems become shared and not just theirs alone.

4. Time management

If you're having trouble getting your child to do things when they need to, it's a good idea to put them in charge of time management – both their own timekeeping and watching out for others keeping to time. They love to be in the role of 'boss', especially of older siblings or parents. And delegate: enlist their help in suggesting solutions to problems and give them responsibility for trying them out. Sometimes, what stands in the way of a solution to time issues is parents who also like to win and want things done their way and *only* their way.

5. Sibling rivalry

One of the difficulties of parenting a B&C child within a family is that they frequently upset siblings either intentionally – to prove their power – or unintentionally, through their demanding and egotistical behaviour. It's important for

all family members to feel valued for their individual qualities and actions, and, therefore, to make sure that each of
them frequently praises the other and shares in the other's
successes. With a strong family identity, the B&C child can
actually feel that the accomplishment of a sibling reflects
well on them too.

Given the B&C child's tendency to dominate, it's a good
idea to ensure that all children get some quality one-to-one
time. It's also important that everyone's good experiences are
shared with the family, rather than just concentrating on
those whose exploits are the most memorable or are told the
best. The B&C child can be encouraged to listen by being
praised for their attentiveness, and even by being asked for
their thoughts on how well so and so did (if being silent is
too taxing for them).

Questions and answers

Q. *My child is away on school trip right now and will be
having a fabulous time. The trouble will come when she gets
home and there will be at least twenty-four hours of hell before
she settles back into the family. I'm dreading it and feel quite
guilty that it's been so peaceful without her.*
A. The B&C child wants to be the centre of attention and
doesn't like having to share the limelight. So when they have
had a particularly exciting time, they will want to go on
enjoying the experience when they return; the crushing sense
of anticlimax on arrival back home (with the added pressure
of knowing that – whether or not they articulate the
thought – others within the family may have enjoyed a peaceful week too) may make them more than usually difficult.

The best plan is probably to allow her to be the focus of
attention when she gets home, and make a clear public

statement from the rest of the family that we are 'glad to have you back'.

Try to involve everyone in the homecoming and in thinking about how to make her feel welcomed back. Talk with the others about how to do this and incorporate as many suggestions as possible. Perhaps you could make a special cake to mark the occasion, choose one of her favourite foods for supper, allow everyone an extra half-hour on their bedtime to share in the homecoming experience or try a game to encourage sharing of feelings. Make it a real family night. Give credit where due for each idea to enhance the sense of inclusion: 'The balloons were Rowan's idea'; 'Elliot made the banner'. And urge the others to listen to your daughter's experiences and ask her questions.

Thereafter, while it's good to listen to her experiences, encourage your child to dwell on the trip herself and to write it down. Perhaps you could buy her a scrapbook she can put photos in or cut out pictures from handouts and stick them in too. And rather than constantly checking on her progress, wait for the finished result – that way the motivation to finish it comes from her. Also, whatever stage it gets taken to, suggest that she shows it to Grandma or your next-door neighbour, as a record of something she really enjoyed.

Q. *My B&C child's siblings tend to gang up on him and I often feel sorry for him. It can't feel very good when everyone rounds on him at the same time and he must feel isolated.*
A. The problem with siblings ganging up is that it actually reinforces the child's position as the 'special one' and their isolation may seem even more justified to them. They can take a certain pride in being different; being the oddball. The more they are told how ghastly they are, the more they feel that this is their role within the family. This easily translates in an adolescent to being 'misunderstood' and unappreciated too.

In the long run, as an ideal to aim at, it's a good idea to stress family unity and how what makes one member happy or unhappy individually also affects the others. A family is a unit and there should not be rifts between the members.

Take time to talk to all your children, one-to-one, about the 'ganging up'. Get them to tell you honestly the things that annoy them, and see if you can work with them to find ways in which they can deal with the irritations without resorting to bullying.

Q. *This emphasis on 'one-to-one' time with the child is all very well, but it makes me feel a bit left out when it's my partner who's doing it. He gets all the good bits of our B&C child by doing nice things with him, and I get the difficult behaviour when they come home again.*

A. Everyone needs some one-to-one time to feel valued, and you have to make sure you're getting yours with both your partner and your child. Try to see the one-to-one time your partner spends with your child as being in the long-term interests of both the child and the entire family's harmony, rather than taking away from the time you could have enjoyed together.

You really need to spend some time talking to your partner about this, and looking at ways of ensuring that supporting your child's development is an equal priority for each of you, even if you carry out different roles.

We suspect that the reason you are on the receiving end of difficult behaviour when they get home is that you want your partner's attention and your child wants yours. Find a way to give your child all the attention they crave for a short period when they get in, then make sure that you and your partner have the rest of the evening for some quality time by yourselves.

3

WHY BOTHER?

Potential Problems for a Bright and Challenging Child

CHAPTER SNAPSHOT

In this chapter we'll explore the particular dangers your child may face as they enter adolescence and move on into young adulthood.

We are listing these potential risks not to scare you, but to prepare you. When risks are clear, solutions and strategies for minimising them become more apparent too. We will deal here with the risks that are likely to present themselves first; later in the book, we will help you prepare your child for some of the risks they may face when older (see Chapter 10).

What are the risks?

Essentially, the problem can be defined quite simply – the bright and challenging child becomes independent far too young. Now, you may wonder where the risk lies here. There are many parents of twenty-five-year-olds who are still living at home, and showing no signs of moving on, who may be at a loss to understand why anyone should be concerned if their child wants to try their wings as soon as they're able.

But the truth is that for the B&C child, this desire for independence can come far too soon: before they are able to see what is really happening around them; before they are able to appreciate the consequences of their actions; and before they have the skills to manage and negotiate their way through difficult situations. They have a tendency to try to 'run before they can walk' in many areas of life. And because they seem so able and mature, parents often let them make decisions for themselves that they would not allow their less articulate children to make.

But while they may present supreme confidence, your child is no more capable of manoeuvring their way through difficult situations than any other young person of their age. They lack the life experience to match their self-belief and verbal and cognitive abilities. They are no more streetwise than anyone else of their age, and may well be less so – depending on their upbringing.

There are some specific risk factors that all young people growing up today face, and these are exacerbated in the case of the B&C child. The main ones almost certainly include:

- alcohol
- early sexual activity
- drugs
- weapons
- money
- social exclusion

Also:

- lack of sleep
- emotional health

- mental health
- lack of interest in education

Let's look at each of these to see how the B&C child may be at particular risk. We will examine them all now, but some we will return to in greater detail later on.

Alcohol

Because the B&C child is the one who will do everything early and to excess if it gets them attention, they will possibly start drinking alcohol from a young age. And because they are resourceful and clever they will probably be able to get it quite easily; whether that involves sneaking it out of the house when you're not watching, or using their silver tongues to persuade other people to buy it for them.

By the time such a child reaches puberty, the attention of their peers has almost entirely taken over their field of vision: your attention or that of other adults such as teachers or strangers is no longer of great value to them. While they will still play to any crowd, their preferred audience will always be other young people. So they will try to impress, to shock, to gain approval, demonstrate bravado and generally get themselves noticed by their use of alcohol.

The risks of alcohol are well known to most adults. For young people, by far the biggest risks are the exploitation and abuse that can come with alcohol: too much renders a young person vulnerable to the behaviour of others. A twelve-year-old who has had too much to drink is not only at risk from the effects of the alcohol itself – and too much in one go will kill – they are also vulnerable to sexual advances, aggression, violence and errors of judgement that can be harmful or even life-threatening. From walking on high walls to swimming in rough seas, actions that may have an element of risk at any time become very dangerous indeed when alcohol is involved.

CASE STUDY

Ten-year-old Rufus is at school, having a lesson on alcohol. The children in his class are looking at different alcoholic drinks and comparing their alcohol content. Rufus goes along the table of empty bottles saying loudly, 'I like that; I like that; I love that; that's too sweet,' and so on, with every item on show.

Rufus may or may not have tried these drinks, but he is using the situation to get attention from peers by showing that he thinks the experience of alcohol on a wide scale is a desirable thing.

The teacher, understanding the reasons why Rufus is behaving in this way, chooses not to challenge him in front of his peers, but to set an example to the other children by ignoring him. However, she takes him aside later and asks him about the drinks he claims to have had, and, with a notebook on her lap and a pen in her hand, prepares to write down what he says. She then asks him when, where and in whose company these things have happened and he immediately begins to back down.

She then warns him against making claims that might get both himself and others into trouble and he agrees to let the matter rest.

Early sexual activity

In keeping with their tendency to experiment and push themselves, B&C children may well be sexually precocious when they hit adolescence. Flirting, sexual behaviour and sexual attractiveness provide another arena in which they can show all and sundry how fabulous and irresistible they are. This leads them to be vulnerable to those who want to exploit young people for sex, and particularly vulnerable to being 'groomed' by adults who can rationalise and use logic to support their intentions – after all, these children are suckers for a good, logical explanation in which they are praised for their rationality and maturity of thought.

They may also get hooked on the attention-grabbing elements of sex – particularly girls who get showered with attention and compliments by young men looking for sex. Or they may mistake their ability to find sexual partners as a validation of their attractiveness, rather than a result of their sexual behaviour and choices. They may find themselves suffering emotionally for all their easy sexual activity, which may not, in any case, give them the sense of adoration they seek. In fact, they may feel desperate at just being wanted as a short-term sexual partner and being rejected over and over again.

By and large B&C children (when young people) will be relatively good at using contraception, as they understand the need for it if they choose not to have a pregnancy. However, for some, pregnancy provides the 'look-at-me' factor they crave, particularly if friends or schoolmates have been showered in attention for pregnancy or having a child.

While they may take care of contraception, they are not generally so good at negotiating safer sex and condom use. The process of negotiating without having a specific aim in mind is not something they are used to and the discussion of condoms and the using of them may seem distasteful or even overly intimate (the B&C child tends not to be strong on intimacy). This leads the sexually active young person to be at risk of sexually transmitted infections.

Example

During a PSHE lesson at a primary school, a year six class were asked to work in small groups and to compile a list of the qualities and characteristics they considered important in a potential boyfriend or girlfriend.

Eleven-year-old Annabel insisted that her group add 'good in bed' to the list of qualities even though at least two or three of the group were embarrassed or didn't understand.

When the list was read out to the class it caused a lot of giggling from some group members and lots of talk followed in the playground as all the children tried to establish who had made the comment.

The teacher considered that the point had been made to 'show off' to the other children and to draw attention to herself and so chose not to pursue it further although she mentioned it as an example of precocious sexual knowledge to the school's Child Protection Officer.

Drugs

There are many reasons why young people take drugs. It may be for recreation or fun, to alter their reality, to ease emotional pain, to overcome social awkwardness and inhibitions, to enhance experience, to push back the boundaries – or any combination of these factors. And, of course, these reasons may apply to any young person.

But the B&C child is more at risk due to aspects of their profile, such as:

- their need for attention from peers
- their belief that they are already perfectly capable of 'taking care' of themselves, regardless of age
- their desire to stand out in a crowd
- their need to be seen as bold and unafraid

Add to this the unshakeable belief held by many young people that no harm can come to them, and that they will be able to handle the consequences of their choices, and there is reason to be concerned.

By far the most common first experience of drugs for most young people will be cigarettes. The B&C child may start to smoke well before most of their peers – possibly even at primary school.

If anyone else in the family smokes, the risk of this is even higher, as they will have an opportunity to take the odd cigarette from a parent's pack unnoticed – and, of course, their parents are less likely to notice the smell of cigarette smoke on them.

On the other hand, some B&C children may take an equally strong line against smoking, being precociously packed with opinions on the risks and dangers to health and keen to tell those who do smoke how foolish they are (and most likely to friends and relatives of your age rather than theirs).

You will probably know already what your child's opinions on smoking are, as they will rarely keep an opinion to themselves. Beware though, many children who are vociferous about the dangers of tobacco change when they get older and start to see things differently; and when smoking becomes more trendy. Just because they have regaled you and anyone within earshot with their thoughts on the evils of smoking in the past doesn't mean that they will continue to think that way.

As an early smoker, the B&C child may feel cool and get a lot of notice from peers (even though much of it may be critical). They may even begin to get a reputation for being a bit wild or daring, which they will enjoy immensely and which may well encourage them to keep up the image.

A similar pattern may follow with other drug use: experimenting early and making sure that others know about it to feed their 'wild child' reputation.

Example

When the class is asked to design and make a poster featuring an international symbol, nine-year-old Ryan produces a 'Keep off the grass' poster featuring a red circle with a line through it across a clearly identifiable cannabis leaf. The teacher displays it with the other posters on the class wall.

Although it is unlikely Ryan has actually seen a cannabis leaf (unless a family member had grown one), he clearly knows what one looks like. What is clear is that Ryan is 'showing off' his knowledge in a way that is designed to make fun of his teacher and to prove his superior knowledge to his classmates.

Weapons

We are constantly hearing terrible news of young people involved in knife and gun crimes. It seems to have taken on almost epidemic proportions, and there are even reports of young people found carrying screwdrivers and other household tools and implements for use as weapons. It's easy to believe that these events are mainly found in large estates and other areas where territorial gangs operate. And while this may be true in many instances, most parents would be horrified to realise how many young people from all areas regularly carry weapons, even to school. Nor is the trend just confined to boys – many girls carry a weapon too.

Like all the risks we're outlining, the reasons for carrying weapons are varied and individual. Fear, aggression and sticking up for oneself seem to be the main reasons given by young people – it's better to be prepared than to be a victim. But what they often don't realise is that carrying a weapon may well mean that a young person is *more* not less likely to get hurt themselves.

The reasons why a B&C child may be drawn to carrying

a weapon are similar to the reasons why they are drawn to any risky behaviour – many of their peers will be impressed, and they may gain status and kudos by being seen to be 'hard' or 'lethal' by others. Of course, as with so many of the other risk factors to which children are drawn, it only works in their favour as long as they are in the minority. As they get older, and more and more of their peers follow suit, then they will need to go further and further to prove their pack-leader position.

Example
Eleven-year-old Daisy is a typical B&C child. Small for her age and ostracised from most of her peer group for her uncompromising desire to win at everything, she regularly carries a 3-inch vegetable knife in her boot or sock, even to school. She shows it to some others at school and word gets round that she is hard and rather crazy. Everyone knows of her and she has a reputation for having a fierce and uncontrollable temper, which, in combination with the knife, means many of the young people at her school give her a wide berth.

But while her peers steer clear, several of the older pupils, particularly the boys, take to her as a bit of a mascot and she basks in being seen around with this group of much older and tougher students. They take delight in winding her up and seeing her reactions, particularly when it involves one of her peers.

Daisy has found a way to get the attention and approval that she thinks single her out from a group of much older students. To her this is a result, as she is now 'in' with the big, tough lads of her school. However, as they are constantly trying to get her to react and act out against others for their amusement, Daisy could well go too far and actually use the knife she carries (or come up against someone else with a knife who uses it against her). As she gets older and grows, her novelty value will start to wane; she may feel compelled to behave in more and more outrageous ways to get the attention of others.

Money

Somewhere in each B&C child's early history lie the seeds of what they will choose to use to get their fix of attention and reinforcement. For many, these are the things that money can buy.

Boys, in particular, get kudos from having all the latest gadgets and gizmos – games consoles, phones, MP3 players, even jackets with built-in speakers in the hood! If these things stand out from the crowd, and are seen as desirable by their peer group, the B&C child may well want them passionately. Also, when they get a new item they may stay up night and day until they have it mastered, so that they can be the first to reach 'Level 6' or whatever is considered to be top of the pile.

For girls, fashion will often suggest the 'must-have' items: the newest cut of jeans (or designer brand), the latest shoes or bag, the 'in' hairstyle – any or all of these may be their way of outdoing everyone else. Many young women are happy to have their clothes from high-street stores, but if this is the case, the B&C girl will want every 'must-have' item as soon as it hits the shelf, so they can be the first to wear it, and declare that everyone else who buys it subsequently is 'copying' them.

And both boys and girls can find themselves wanting more, more and still more of everything.

Gill once did a project in a boys' secondary school on students who were not seen to be fitting in well with their peers in their first year. Pupils who make a poor transition, such as these lads – at a time considered to be a very important period in a child's life – are known to be statistically more at risk of almost everything from bullying to truancy, drug and alcohol misuse and anti-social behaviour than their peers. Gill asked each of the boys to prepare a brief introduction about himself and to deliver it to the group, so that they could all get to know each other a bit. Each of them in turn got up and recited a catalogue of possessions – they listed video games, electronic equipment such as DVD players and computers (by make and model in some cases) as well as designer-label trainers and clothing. There was no mention of individual qualities or tastes; they were all defining themselves simply in terms of what they had and, in so doing, they were demonstrating their place within the new group by showing their similarity to each other, while vying for status in trying to outdo each other too. It was hardly surprising that this group had found it difficult to make new friendships with peers and form good relationships with adults, as their only way to relate to each other was by trying to impress through material 'wealth'.

The problem for any young person who makes possessions a way of getting themselves noticed is money – they may not have as much as they would like in order to finance the purchases they need to stay newsworthy. So they may become unhealthily focused on costs and money: who spent what; who earned what; what something cost. They may even begin to look at ways of getting money quickly. This could mean a paper round or putting pressure on a parent to be paid for help around the house, or it can mean something far less healthy such as supplying cannabis to peers or selling household items they think no one will miss. We've even heard of a nine-year-old girl who was renting out her family's collection of DVDs at £1 per item per week. (We heard the story from the girl's mother, who was astonished at her daughter's resourcefulness and decidedly proud of her entrepreneurial spirit – exactly what a B&C child would want.)

While we may applaud a child for their resourcefulness, we would consider it a concern if a child used shared family property without permission to make money for themselves alone.

Example

At his primary school, eleven-year-old Connor is discovered running a gambling game during playtimes that involves guessing the total number of 'spots' shown on two rolled dice. The winner gets their stake doubled and the thrower (i.e. Connor) takes the rest of the losing bets. The bets are small – only one or two pence mostly, but he is found to be taking over £2 a day from his peers, some of whom are becoming quite hooked on the game, even stealing small amounts from parents to be able to play.

This is a typical B&C story. Connor has used his intellect and organisational ability to get what he wants – money. He has also got the attention of his peers and a starring role in his mini casino business. Plus, his parents, though shocked, will be telling the story with a hint of pride and a lot of amusement for years to come.

Social exclusion

The B&C child always walks a tightrope between being adored and being reviled by their family and peers. Their attention-seeking behaviour can win them many fans as they often embody the behaviour their more inhibited peers would like to exhibit themselves. Their wit and humour, coupled with their quick thinking, make them great fun to be around much of the time. However, the downside is that they never know when enough is enough. When people tire of them and their cleverness and attention-seeking they are likely to up the ante and become even more vociferous and obnoxious, more animated and exuberant and more attention-seeking. Most B&C children have yet to learn that what can be amusing in small doses can quickly become annoying when it goes too far or goes on for too long.

As a consequence, some such children find themselves with very few, if any, real friends as they get older. They may have plenty of people they can spend time with and chat to, but few people they are comfortable with for hours on end and who are comfortable with them in return. It is not uncommon to find B&C teens who are very much alone at school and may even find themselves being somewhat isolated at home too as siblings grow older and spend more time with their own friendship group. Sometimes they team up with other young people with similar interests, but such an arrangement seldom works well, as a truly B&C child will remain deeply competitive within any relationship.

The risks that accompany social exclusion are many, but may include dangerous attention-seeking behaviour such as refusing food or extreme dieting leading to anorexia, creating false fantasy dramas with themselves at the heart of the tragedy (a dying parent, an incurable disease, a missing sibling, etc.) or an extreme reaction to a topical issue. For instance, exaggerated grief at the death of a movie star or figure from popular culture, taking an extreme stance in relation to a news item or becoming obsessed with a religious group or political party whose views differ dramatically from those of family and peers. So the child of staunch Labour supporters may well become an arch Young Conservative, the child of liberal parents may well develop extreme racist views and the child of Christian parents may declare their intention to become a Muslim or vice versa.

The real risk here is that the B&C child may lose themselves somewhere in all this. Their fragile self-esteem may be dented by the lack of approval and affirmation from others and the constant veering from one extreme reaction to another may lead them to lose touch with reality – leaving them feeling lost and alone. From here, feelings of depression and self-loathing may lead to a worsening spiral of erratic behaviour over which they have no control.

Example
Twelve-year-old Marina's parents dealt with her attention-seeking behaviour by ignoring her. She became more and more desperate to win, and after getting into a lot of trouble at school for stealing, bullying and lying, grew isolated from her peers and disliked by teachers at the school.

She began to refuse food when she was ten, as a way of forcing her parents to focus on her, which they did, making her more and more determined not to eat. She became ill with anorexia and was referred to specialist services. However, being around other young people with eating disorders brought out her competitive streak, so that she had to be the 'sickest' or thinnest of them all.

At secondary school, she gained a certain cachet for her eating disorder, and staff treated her more kindly than at primary school, but she began to make up outrageous stories to gain their sympathy and care. She told everyone that she was thin because she had cancer and was dying and that her mother had also died of the same thing only a year before. When the school checked with her family, realised her story was untrue and challenged her, she took an overdose of paracetamol and had to be hospitalised.

Marina's is an extreme case of what can happen when a B&C child loses their place in their family and peer group. Her social exclusion was, of course, partly her own doing, but her attempts at improving things for herself only made them worse, as she lacked the skills and self-awareness to understand the consequences of her choices.

Other risks

Not all of the risks to your child's health, happiness and wellbeing are as serious as those we've just looked at. Other risks include:

- **Lack of sleep.** B&C children are notorious for being unwilling to go to bed, and for staying awake half the night when they do

- **Emotional health.** When a child is particularly verbally able, it often follows that people assume that the other aspects of the child are equally developed. Just because a child can talk about anything and everything in a mature and adult way does not mean that their ability to recognise, deal with and appropriately express their emotions is equally developed. In fact it is often the case that children who 'pretend' to be adult much of the time will avoid expressions of emotion as 'childish'. In consequence they may not develop the same level of emotional resilience and ease of expression as their more 'trial and error' peers. This may begin to be apparent in their early teens when they display the kind of extreme reactions often seen in very young children, such as tantrums or suffocating displays of affection

- **Mental health.** There is no suggestion that a bright and challenging child is any more at risk of mental health issues than any other child. However, there is much evidence that suggests that misusing drugs and substances regularly, particularly from a young age, may have mental health implications for some

- **Dropping out of school.** They may get disenchanted with school and feel unappreciated and bored. These days, there is more awareness of the needs of able pupils, but some still fall through the system, particularly if they have unconventional interests and skills

- **Trouble with the law.** There are two main kinds of problem here. The bright child who is underachieving may well get into anti-social behaviour, such as smashing up a bus shelter as a way of getting attention from peers or expressing frustration. They might also get into trouble with the law by trying to outwit the system – Stephen Fry, for example (now a national treasure for his extreme intelligence, wit and eloquence), was arrested and imprisoned when young for credit card fraud. So they may become hackers, computer virus makers, tricksters or con artists who use their intelligence to outwit others, and view their cleverness as justification for the crime

- **Bullying.** Either as perpetrator or victim. B&C children don't like to be outdone or ignored and may respond spitefully to someone who uses either strategy on them. They can be powerful enemies, as they have a great talent for finding their opponents' weak spots and can use their superior verbal ability and intellect to cause maximum hurt. On the other hand, they can also be vulnerable to bullying, as their transparent attention-seeking or eccentric behaviour will upset and annoy others

- **Running away or leaving home early.** Most young people who run away from home do so for a reason that seems compelling to them, but almost certainly without realising the dangers and uncertainties that homelessness will present. The B&C child may well use 'running away' as a way of punishing parents for their behaviour; a means of trying to get control. They may not go far – they may just stay with a friend for a few days, or a grandparent or relative if there is one living close by – until they are lured home by having their conditions met

- **Taking physical risks.** The B&C child is a sucker for a dare, or, even more powerful, the 'I bet you can't' challenge from peers. Anything that allows them to outshine their peer group or become the centre of attention and gossip will appeal. They may well attempt to climb higher, jump further, swing longer or escape faster than others, sometimes with tragic consequences

The biggest risk to the B&C child

The biggest risk to the bright and challenging child is that those parenting them give up: tired out with the effort of trying, they take refuge in their child's assertive confidence; they decide that perhaps the child can make their own decisions and just leave them to get on with it. This may sound tempting if you are an exhausted parent, worn down by constant assertiveness and lacking the confidence in your own ability to see things straight. If this is how you feel, the remainder of this book offers support. But a withdrawal of parenting is the last thing that your child needs.

REFLECTION EXERCISE

No parent likes to think that their young child is likely to take drugs, to engage in early sexual activity or to be prey to any other of the risks discussed in this chapter. This exercise will help you to overcome that hurdle in the interests of preparing your child for the possible pitfalls ahead.

Look at each of the risk elements outlined below and, using your knowledge of your child, give a score for each item listed from 0 (meaning no risk whatsoever) to 5 (meaning a high risk).

Remember, we are not talking about this year or even the next two or three, perhaps – we are considering the risks your child may be susceptible to when they hit their early teens.

Alcohol?	0	1	2	3	4	5
Early sexual activity?	0	1	2	3	4	5
Drugs?	0	1	2	3	4	5
Weapons?	0	1	2	3	4	5
Money?	0	1	2	3	4	5
Social exclusion?	0	1	2	3	4	5
Lack of sleep?	0	1	2	3	4	5
Emotional health?	0	1	2	3	4	5
Mental health?	0	1	2	3	4	5
Lack of interest in education?	0	1	2	3	4	5
Trouble with the law?	0	1	2	3	4	5
Bullying?	0	1	2	3	4	5
Running away from home?	0	1	2	3	4	5

Once you have assessed the likely risks take a look at any you have given a 3 or higher.

What, if anything, can you do to make your child better informed, better prepared or less at risk of harm in this hazardous area? For example, if you have identified them as being at a risk level 3 from mental health issues because of their extreme temper, you might choose to research anger-management techniques so that you are in a better position to help them learn to control their temper.

Things I can do to reduce the risk of harm for my child include:

_____

_____

_____

_____

_____

_____

_____

This is not an easy exercise but it is an important one. All children are at risk of some things in our modern world but where you live, who they spend time with, their temperament and interests may make them more at risk of some things than others. A high proportion of smoking parents will have kids who go on to smoke, your mother's age when she had her first child is a risk factor for teenage pregnancy and poor diet and exercise habits are often copied from parents too.

CASE STUDY

Marion was only fifteen when she had her son Lewis, who is now twelve. Marion is aware that he is physically quite advanced for his age and is becoming more and more interested in girls and sexual imagery. As a single parent, Marion is also aware that Lewis lacks a positive male role model or mentor to guide him in his development as a sexually mature male. The reflection exercise above helped her to establish that Lewis is at risk of early sexual activity and the resulting emotional and physical risks that may bring – not least, that of becoming an early parent himself.

Marion decided to support her son by enlisting the help of his uncle, who he was close to and asking him to develop their relationship to include discussions around sex and sexual behaviour, as well as finding out how she could provide a good education for her son. She looked up her nearest Speakeasy course for parents (see Resources, p. 271) and started to become more confident in talking about sex with him herself.

Questions and answers

Q. *My daughter insists on dressing in clothing that is both provocative and sexual – and yet she is only ten. If I try to tell her of the kind of attention she risks attracting, she tells me I am out of date and boring. How can I encourage her to listen to me?*

A. You cannot make a ten-year-old understand an adult point of view, because, quite simply, she's a child. She does not have the life experience to see it from your perspective, nor does she understand the sexual nature of adults and how it can influence behaviour. She also cannot understand sexual risk – she's only ten.

However, you are right and she is wrong. She may be at risk if she dresses inappropriately, and your job as a parent is to make the decisions that will keep her safe, not to try to get her to make them when they are simply not in her sphere of understanding. For now on, you must take a stand, even if it is unpopular. Maybe you are old-fashioned, but your child's safety has to come first. Put your foot down and make the decisions you need to make. As she gets older and has more understanding of the possible consequences of her choices, she can start to make her own decisions.

Q. *My son stays out late, and, although only twelve, he regularly comes home on his own, after eleven. He says he does not need sleep and is convinced he can take care of himself. What should I do?*
A. You have already allowed him too much freedom. Twelve is far too young an age to be staying out so late without adult supervision, and sleep is the last of my concerns for him. If he's doing this now where will he be in three years' time?

It sounds as though you are trying to reason with him to get him to make another decision rather than being a responsible parent by insisting on a realistic curfew.

It's your choice here. At twelve he is vulnerable to all kinds of influences, and you are being irresponsible in letting him make all his own decisions. He may be mature for his age, but he has still had only a few years' experience of the world and is entering a very crucial phase in his development. Unless you rein him in now, you will not be able to influence his behaviour at all in the future. If he is to grow up safely and negotiate his way through the trials of adolescence, he needs to slow right down now.

So, set a curfew for him that feels appropriate to his age –
perhaps 9 p.m. on weekdays and 10 p.m. at the weekend,
with an understanding that if he sticks to his curfew, you will
be willing to let him stay out even later for special events, as
long as he allows you or another adult to bring him home.

If he misses his curfew, you need to withdraw privileges
and favours from him. Don't give him a lift for a week, no
matter what the circumstances are, refuse him money or
treats above his basic allowance, stop doing his laundry (if
you still do it) or reminding him what he needs to take to
school each day. Don't top up his phone if you usually do.

Make sure he understands that these benefits are being
withdrawn as a direct consequence of him breaking the
curfew, that they are a privilege you choose to give him
(rather than his right) and that they will be restored as soon
as he accepts his curfew and operates within it.

Q. *I worry about drugs and want to talk about the risks to my
son, but he tells me he knows more than I do because it is cov-
ered at school. Can I assume this is right and leave it to them?*
A. Why not ask him to teach you? That way you can learn
more, he can show you how much he knows and you can
prompt him to think things through by asking some
thought-provoking questions as part of the learning process.
To get you started, and avoid the eye contact you might both
find embarrassing, why not look together at some of the
excellent websites that offer drugs information (see p. 273).

4

IT'S NOT FAIR!

Boundary Setting and Saying 'No'

CHAPTER SNAPSHOT

This chapter will outline the importance of boundaries in parenting – and in particular the importance of boundaries to the B&C child. Unless these are set and maintained now, your child will be almost impossible to rein back in once they become older and beyond any adult's ability to manage. This, in combination with a lack of life experience, will make them vulnerable: at risk of harm and making poor life choices.

You will also find some tips here on how to set boundaries and deal with the flak that ensues, as well as guidance on what to do if your child oversteps them.

What is a boundary?

A boundary is a new name for the oldest principle of parenting there is – what you do and do not allow in relation to your child's behaviour.

There are boundaries upon all of us all the time – some set up by law such as a speed limit on the road or not smoking in restaurants and pubs, some by social convention such as not pointing and laughing at a stranger in the street whose appearance is unusual, and there are family boundaries, such as going to bed at eight-thirty when you are eight years old, or not being allowed to play out in the street.

Boundaries can be fixed (such as laws), or changeable due to circumstance or setting. So, for instance, making fun of the way someone speaks would generally be considered rude, but between good friends it might be regarded as funny and acceptable (particularly if an individual makes a joke about themselves first, and so indicates that it's OK to laugh about it).

We also have boundaries we place upon ourselves. Mostly these relate to our values, morals and beliefs – for example, not swearing, or giving everyone an equal say in conversation. Boundaries like these, that are almost part of who we are, seldom need any reinforcement. Most of the time, we stick to them automatically, and may even consider them to be a part of our personality rather than values-based boundaries.

Occasionally, we set boundaries on ourselves using our thought processes alone: boundaries of the 'From now on . . .' type. So, we may say, 'From now on, I'm only going to eat chocolate at weekends', or, 'From now on, I'm only going to drink alcohol when I go out', or even, 'I'm going to get up an hour earlier every morning and go for a run'. Unless these come from a deeply held belief – about ourselves, our lives or our needs – they will probably last a very short time before they are swept away; indeed most New Year's resolutions are broken by the end of January. However, when someone has had a serious health scare they find it easy to keep to a new exercise regime, or if a person has experienced shame or embarrassment from an action, a resolution never to repeat it may be kept without difficulty.

Children are much the same. They will make promises

based on their thought processes – what they think they should do or think is the right answer – but this will not automatically translate into a change of behaviour unless the need for that change is attached to a personal experience, a moral or value or a deeply held belief. So it's up to adults to make boundaries for children: to help them keep healthy, behave appropriately in a range of settings and keep them safe.

Setting boundaries is one thing, but making sure they are adhered to is another. There's one vital principle to grasp: the only way you will ever get a child to keep to a boundary is by reinforcing and maintaining it. Setting one, then shrugging your shoulders and raising your eyes to heaven when they break it will neither encourage nor teach a child to respect any of the boundaries placed on them.

We all learn that different people do things in different ways and children learn this too. It may well be that the behaviour Grandma expects in her home differs from the behaviour you expect – and that, in turn, may vary in the homes of their friends. When a child is very small this can be a little confusing, but they soon come to realise that it is normal for things to change from place to place; that most boundaries are not absolutes but 'rules' for behaviour in different settings – and that people have the right to set their own boundaries in their own space.

Some children spend large amounts of time in two different homes. Often, this is because their parents have split up and each now lives an independent life while sharing contact with their child. It will frequently be the case that divided parents will have different boundaries and expectations for their child. Where parents are mature and adult enough to separate the needs of their child from any personal rancour, they will communicate on a regular basis about not only the material issues relating to their shared care such as when to pick them up for the next visit, but also questions of parenting that arise so that a shared approach can be ensured.

Although we have met many parents who have, albeit grudgingly, put personal issues aside for the welfare of their child, we have met many, many others for whom parenting has become a competitive sport between warring factions. Sometimes parents will vie with each other to be the more popular or preferred parent in an unspoken battle to see who can cause the most hurt. Children can only suffer in such circumstances, and parents need to seek professional help if they are unable to maintain a suitable level of emotional care for their child. While we understand that many parents feel bitter and angry at an ex-partner, it is crucial that they keep such feelings out of the relationship with their child. A child has the right to love and be loved by their parents without either feeling guilt or being encouraged to manipulate the guilt or fear of their parents. B&C children are quick to exploit any chink in a parent's defences and a parent who is easily upset by reports of the other parent's wrong- (or right-) doings will be easily led.

Children also come to learn that they have rights over their own space or their own belongings – and are quick to tell anyone who steps over their boundary: 'You are not allowed into my room without asking'; 'You must not take my things.'

Children need adults to set boundaries for them because they are not well equipped to do so for themselves. They simply don't have the experience, understanding or abstract thinking to do so. The most difficult decision for a child to make is one based on future outcomes – especially longer-term ones. So going to bed early because they might be tired tomorrow is simply not a connection a child is capable of making. They will make their decision based solely on how tired they are right now, in the moment of making the decision. They may also have other priorities in mind such as wanting to see something on TV, or feeling they are missing out on the conversation if they go to bed, and these will be far more important to them than any long-term planning.

Even young adults (and, let's face it, all of us) find making decisions based on future consequences as opposed to any short-term gain really hard at times. Otherwise why would anyone smoke, eat or drink too much – or wake up in the morning wishing they could turn the clock back?

Why is it difficult for parents today to set boundaries?

There has been a huge change in the way parents treat their children today, compared with previous generations. Mostly, this is a positive change with children being allowed to develop their own thoughts and feelings, likes and dislikes without being 'controlled' by their parents or other adults. However, many people think that things may have gone a bit too far, and educationalists and others who deal professionally with children and young people are urging a return to some of the more traditional methods of parenting.

At the same time, more and more parents are feeling lost and overwhelmed by their role, uncertain as to what they should or should not do for their child's wellbeing. In part, this is a product of their feelings about the way in which they themselves were parented, and many of them will remember swearing that they would do things differently with their own children. We both grew up in the 1950s and '60s, when it was quite normal to tell a child exactly what to do, even how to stand and what to say when someone spoke to us.

But whereas this prescriptive attitude to children's behaviour seemed too controlling at the time, now, with hindsight and some reflection, many of today's parents can see how some of the boundaries that their parents put in place were,

in fact, helpful or necessary (even if it took them a long time
to see why) and that perhaps their fear of putting boundaries
on their own children is misplaced.

Too much control over a child's behaviour can have an
impact on their sense of self and their level of confidence.
But there does have to be a framework for behaviour. Today
we meet children of six who have no set bedtime, choose
what they eat and have televisions in their bedrooms, so they
can watch whatever they want, late into the night. Is it any
wonder that inter-personal skills among children are declin-
ing, that children are frequently too tired to concentrate in
school and that obesity is becoming a national scandal?
Young children know what they like, but they don't know
what is good for them or what is helpful to their development. They make their choices based entirely on pleasure
and the moment they are in. It's up to the older generation to
make choices for them and with them.

So, yes – you do need to set boundaries for your children,
but you also owe it to them to explain why you are doing it.
They may not agree with it or like it, but at least as they get
older, they will understand that it was done in their best
interests.

Many children make a big show of resisting boundaries
and, as they get older, of breaking them. However, boundaries to a young child equal love. A child without boundaries
feels unsure and is often desperate for approval. They may
behave in ways that leave them open to criticism or rejection
from others and therefore they can become unhappy and
insecure. Likewise, a child who is allowed to do as they
please may feel that their parent simply doesn't care and will
push away until they get a stop sign. If this doesn't come
(even if they've had a dozen 'Let's consider this for a
moment' conversations), they will feel directionless and
unsupported.

Understanding choices

We have spoken to some parents who feel that it is only by allowing children to make their own choices and decisions that they will learn to do so in future. While we agree with this in principle, we think that the choices they are allowed to make entirely alone, those in which they are allowed some input and those that should be made on their behalf all need to be carefully considered. The best way to learn is by making simple choices first, before moving on to more complex decision making.

Here is an exercise for you to reflect on making choices for yourself.

REFLECTION EXERCISE

Here is a list of choices:

Put a 1 by the easiest choice for you to make, 2 by the next and so on. Number 5 will correspond to the hardest choice.

a. Choose a video in the video store for the whole family to watch ☐

b. Leave a job you hate even if you don't have another to go to ☐

c. Watch a good programme on TV and so go to bed much later than usual on a work day ☐

d. Tell someone what you think of them or put up with being irritated by their behaviour ☐

e. Chocolate ice cream or strawberry ice cream? ☐

Feedback

There are no wrong answers here; however, there are more frequent ones. The most common order is:

$$a = 3, b = 4/5, c = 2, d = 4/5, e = 1$$

Most people will say that choice b, leaving a job without one to go to or choice d, telling someone what you think of them are the ones they would least like to make. The ability to make the choices proposed often depends on the economic status of the individual: the principal earners in a family tend to feel less inclined to take a risk relating to income than those who have less financial responsibility.

Why are these choices different?

The easiest – choice e – is simply a question of taste; liking one more than another. After all, you can always change your mind straight afterwards and have the other one! No one else will be affected by your choice and there are no long-term consequences to it.

The next – choice c – affects no one but yourself directly, although others may have to deal with the consequences of your tiredness tomorrow. This choice has a slightly further-reaching consequence than the ice cream one, but is still minor.

Then comes choice a. This affects everyone in the family, and may have long-term consequences in terms of both the video that is chosen and the resulting reputation/blame/praise for the person who did the choosing. With this choice comes a high degree of responsibility and the possibility of emotional repercussions.

In shared final position, the consequences for choices b and d are completely unknown. Depending on the decision made over choice b, the whole family could be adversely affected and its security undermined in the future if another job is not forthcoming. For choice d, the consequences are emotional rather than financial, but could still be catastrophic for relationships in the future. Your decision as to which one you put in final place depends on which scares you more: financial or emotional fallout?

The point here is that children must learn complex skills before they are able to make real choices about issues that may affect them for years to come, or even the rest of their lives. They have to understand the impact that their choices have on others – and whether they have the right to make choices that have a clear impact on others, without taking their views into consideration as well. These things cannot be done easily – it takes time, maturity and empathy to learn to make choices well. You need to help children learn how to master these skills so that they don't make decisions that may negatively impact on themselves or others in the process.

Children tend to approach all choices as if they were ice cream choices. Even teenagers will still do this, mostly – what they want outweighs any other consideration. It is therefore the responsibility of adults to differentiate – which choices can they make all by themselves, which need simplifying for them and which need an adult to make them?

I once saw a mum in a cake shop with a three-year-old in a pushchair. 'Which cake do you want?' she asked. I was amazed. On what possible grounds does a child of three make such a choice? Taste? How many can they know? And are they able to approximate taste for things they've never had? And what about cost, and what is good for them – or at least less bad for them? Then there's the question of size? And hunger versus time until the next meal? If I was that child I'd have chosen the wonderful wedding cake with all its frilly bits and flowers – and then been upset to be told that it was not included in my choice range after all.

Gill

Small children need options: 'You can have this, this or this.' And parents can make the more important choices and still give the child some say. Likewise, as they get older, it is perfectly appropriate in a café to say, 'You can have hot chocolate to drink or some chocolate to eat, but not both'; or, 'You can have a smoothie with a cookie or a water-based drink with a muffin.'

The B&C child who is not used to having such boundaries put on their choices may well find it hard at first and may argue. But standing firm now will eventually help them to understand the process of making choices.

Making setting boundaries easier
(for you to establish and for them to stick to)

The easiest way to make boundaries more manageable is for you to understand that it is your job to keep your children safe and well rather than make them happy – and to keep telling yourself so!

So when you put a boundary on them for their own good, feel proud of your parenting. It's easier and more popular to let them have it their own way but in the long term they will be a more mature and likeable person for gradually learning the processes involved in making decisions – and being allowed to make their choices only when they can show themselves able to do so.

Then what you have to do is:

- say what you have decided
- explain your reasoning
- say that it is non-negotiable
- stick to this

As they get older, be prepared to negotiate more. So, for instance, rather than having a set bedtime at seven-thirty on a school night with no argument allowed, as you might for an eight-year-old, as your child gets older and feels that they should be allowed to stay up later, be prepared to discuss it with them.

Some children can be very reasonable and will ask for an extra half-hour on their bedtime. Others will go straight for the big time and ask for an hour and a half, or say that they no longer need a bedtime at all. You must decide what is best for your child's wellbeing – but don't be swayed by the 'all my friends' argument. If you need time to think, perhaps to find out what other parents do, then say so and do your research. As a general rule of thumb, first ask them what they want and work from there to a point of compromise. Perhaps they get to stay up fifteen minutes later, but are allowed an extra half-hour reading time once they are in bed; or they get to stay up half an hour later on the under- standing that they get out of bed at first call in the morning or they will go straight back to an earlier bedtime again.

Children are quick to spot a pattern, so if you always agree to half of what they ask, they will up their demands. Be aware of this and try not to be too predictable. If you want to say 'No', do so, but try to encourage a little real reflection and discussion along the way, rather than just refusing outright.

Why setting boundaries with B&C children can be difficult

1. Your own feelings

As we have seen, B&C children know which buttons to press to make you feel awful: 'You don't love me any more';

'I had to do that because you are always out and never give me any time'; 'You are being unfair'; 'You are pushing me too much.'

Sometimes they will even use the weapon that is every parent's nightmare – showing you up in a public place. They will start to yell or scream at you where others can hear or make really hurtful comments in a loud voice. It's hard to be a parent when your child is behaving badly. It can get in the way of what you had expected would happen (a nice day out, for example) and it takes courage to deal with the situation when every impulse is telling you to shut them up by whatever means possible and as quickly as possible, to stop everyone looking at you (and perhaps judging you).

The situation is particularly common with children who, when in the 'tantrum' phase, were bribed or appeased by being given what they wanted. In other words, children who haven't grown out of throwing tantrums because they haven't learnt that they don't work – indeed, for them, they do.

This situation plays on the insecure parent and their upset feelings. It sends you straight back to your own childhood feelings about how it felt when someone said 'No' to you.

Many parents also have a strong image of how they want their child to see them and this can interfere with how they parent.

REFLECTION EXERCISE

How do I want my child to see me?

Answer this question by rating each of the following suggested qualities from 1 (not at all) to 8 (what I want most):

- as an ally
- as fair
- as someone who listens
- as a friend
- as someone they respect
- as popular with them and their friends
- as fun
- as someone who puts limits on what they can and can't do

Feedback

Now take an honest look at your answers. What do they say about you? Are you more concerned with being liked and being a friend than you are with being a guiding and responsible figure?

How does the way you want them to see you impact on the way you behave with your child? Do you give in to them because you want them to like you? Do you allow them to decide what to eat, wear, watch and when to go to bed because you want them to see you as a friend, not a 'boss'? Or are you prepared to be unpopular for a while in order to teach them responsible behaviour and choices?

Giving in to a small child may seem harmless and even kindly but allowing a child to feel in control of their parent or parents will make them difficult to manage as they grow older and need your wisdom and experience to guide them until they have enough to be self-sufficient.

Example

One morning, four-year-old Florence is brought into school half an hour late; she is clearly unwell, and her mother thinks she should be at home, but she wants to come to school and her mother cannot say 'No' to her. She brings Florence in after the official start of school and expects the teacher, while managing another twenty-five four-year-olds, to make the decision for the child – because, 'She tells me she hates me if I make her do something she doesn't want to do.'

2. They simply don't take 'No' for an answer

B&C children feel that if they accept your boundaries, you are winning. So they fight them, renegotiating every boundary to the last detail, doing their level best to challenge as often as possible, in as awkward a social situation as possible (in front of your mother-in-law, for example). They are also very good at choosing the least convenient time for their discussions, say when you are in a hurry or have to meet a deadline.

They always want the last word and resort to a variety of different ploys – maybe charm and eloquence, maybe aggression. How they get you to renegotiate will vary from child to child, but the bottom line is that they won't stop until you give in and pull back on your decision because you are simply tired or weary of argument.

And, of course, the child who has got an adult to change a boundary once by arguing or reasoning then knows that boundaries *are* negotiable, and they will continue to do it.

Example

In the school playground, eight-year-old Josh comes out of school deep in conversation with his friend Orin. He doesn't acknowledge his mum so she chats to Orin's mother. Orin then asks his mum if Josh can come and play and she replies that he can if his mum allows it.

Josh's mum says no, because his grandfather is coming over to help with the garden and he would like to see Josh. A discussion ensues:

'But I can see Grandad when I get home – I'll only be an hour.'

'No, Josh, I think it's best we go now. You can play with Orin another day, but Grandad only comes to tea once in a while.'

'But, Mum, you're going to be busy anyway, and you always say I get in your way. I'll only be an hour.'

'No, really, Josh. Please, let's go. I haven't got time later to come and pick you up, anyway.'

'Maybe Orin's mum could bring me home [Josh turns to face her, beaming] and that way you could have some time with Grandad by yourself because you hardly ever get to spend time with him on your own.'

And Mum says OK. Josh has learnt that by continuing to press, even when presented with logical objections, he can get his own way. Saying 'No' will be even harder for his mother next time.

The magic maybe

The art of saying 'No' relies on one thing and one thing only: it must never be taken back. Regardless of what your child says, or of how reasonable their argument is, or any embarrassment caused, a 'No' must be final and non-negotiable. Once you stick to this rule they will learn – eventually – that they are wasting their time and will change their behaviour. They may not accept this with good grace, but they *will* come to accept it.

When giving an answer to a request you should give one of three answers:

- 'Yes'
- 'No'
- 'Maybe'

You might have another version of the last option –
'Perhaps' or, 'Can I think about it a bit more?' or, 'Let's talk
about it first' – but, in essence, you are signalling a middle
ground where negotiation is possible. (Be aware, however,
that once you have signalled that you are willing to negotiate, they may badger you mercilessly until you give in or
simply buckle under the strain!)

If your automatic response is a quick 'No', which sometimes means 'No' and sometimes means 'Maybe', it's no
wonder that your child keeps on at you until they get what
they want.

You should also be conscious of how often you are saying
the same thing; if your answer becomes too predictable
your child will undoubtedly find a way to use this to their
advantage.

How to ensure that 'no' means 'no'

1. If your child asks you something always take a
   moment to think before saying 'No' (unless they've
   asked the same thing before).
2. When you are sure that you really do want to say
   'No', simply say it with a one-line explanation, for
   example:

   - No, you cannot have sweets so close to mealtimes.
   - No, you cannot buy everything you like as soon
     as you see it. If you still want it in three weeks'
     time you can buy it then.

- No, you can't go and play, you have homework to finish.
- No, you can't wear that dress, it's not suitable for playing in.

If they come back with a smart answer, don't engage in an argument. Simply say, 'I have said "No", and that is not up for negotiation. No means no.' The first few times they'll bluster and shout or sulk, but in the end they will get the point.

3. If you have said no clearly and given your reason, break eye contact to discourage debate and negotiation attempts from them. Try to engage their attention elsewhere as soon as possible so that they are not commanding your undivided attention.

4. Never change your mind once you have said 'No', even if you think you have been too hasty. Once it's been said, all sides must abide by it. You too have to accept the consequences – it's written in stone.

5. If you are unsure, say 'Maybe' and ask for more clarification or a deal to be struck such as:

- 'Maybe you can – what were you thinking of?'
- 'Maybe you can buy it if you have the money, but have you thought about it enough, and what else you might need the money for?'
- 'Maybe you can go and play; can we just talk about how much homework you have, and when it is due?'
- 'Maybe you can wear that dress, but what do you think so and so will think if you do?'

Maybes should not be left hanging. Give them a clear idea when an answer will be forthcoming. For example:

- 'Let's talk about this some more before I decide.'
- 'I need to ask Aunty Alice first; I'll talk to her tomorrow and let you know then.'

6. If you (or your partner or another trusted adult for that matter) have said 'No' to your child and they disregard it, this is a serious breach of the rules and should always be dealt with in a serious manner.
7. When a child has broken a boundary, they have to put things right. The extent of the making right will depend on the boundary that has been broken, but it might include:

- no sweets for a week
- no pocket money for a week
- no going out to play for a week
- not being allowed to wear 'that dress' or 'those trainers' for a week

They will need to be encouraged and in some instances *strongly guided* to come up with a solution. How appropriate their initial suggestion is will have to be discussed. While it may be related to the incident that caused the discussion and what they have done, in many cases there is no obvious way of putting this right. So what is the sanction for a child who has just called his sister a rude name? Getting called one in return? I think not. What he will need to do is make his sister forgive him – probably by apologising or perhaps by something more active like playing with her for half an hour.

What to do if the B&C child won't accept a boundary

If your child has been brought up with almost no imposed boundaries and has pretty much made all their own decisions it will not be easy for them to accept a change in the balance of power. A child who is used to getting their own way will be genuinely outraged at any attempt to impose rules or restrictions upon them. They may well have an image of themselves as being beyond the limits set on others – as many teachers will testify.

When you first try to place a non-negotiable boundary your child will pull out all the stops. They will resist by any number of means, which may include:

- verbal abuse – often of a particularly hurtful and personal kind (Gill is still recovering from the child who called her an 'ugly old woman' a few weeks ago!)
- extreme anger and rage – possibly of the tantrum variety
- breaking things you value or gave to them
- repeating an unfair version of events to a third person (e.g. grandparents, your siblings or your estranged partner)
- stirring things up at home, e.g. creating disharmony among siblings
- making accusations of cruelty against you – possibly to another adult
- taking out their loss of power on a younger or weaker sibling or pet by being physically or emotionally cruel
- picking on, or even bullying, peers in an attempt to prove their power

- sulking with much pouting and sighing and slouching around
- pretending not to hear you and completely ignoring anything you say or, conversely, mimicking and copying everything you say and do

If you have told them they must (or must not) follow a certain course of action and they refuse point-blank to listen, action is needed. Meanwhile, they may show their disapproval in any number of ways, and some of these can be quite frightening in their intensity. Basically, they will attempt to get you to back down through any means.

Once their intention of not complying has been made very clear – however they go about it – give them a simple ultimatum: either they go along with your decision or they will have to accept a simple and immediate consequence.

We would normally recommend that this is to be sent to their room for a period of time; it is not intended to be a horrible punishment – after all, they will have toys and books and plenty of nice things to do there. Rather, it is designed to give them some time alone to think about their behaviour (although they might take a lot longer to get round to that than you might think), and to realise that by not complying with expectations they are being temporarily excluded from the family unit and family life (though never, of course, from the love of their family). They may choose to rejoin at any stage by doing whatever has been asked of them. They don't have to say sorry – B&C children find this almost impossible on occasion as it implies they have done something wrong and they will seldom accept they have. They do not need to discuss their behaviour or hold a post-mortem – they simply have to do as asked. As soon as they do, immediately let them feel your approval and that all is over and done with.

If yours is a really stubborn child, for whom winning

against parents is everything, you may have to arrange the support of a go-between to have a word with them; or if they'll talk, you may need to talk to them yourself, but wait until their anger has cooled down. The part of the brain in which anger is experienced is not the same as the one where reason and logic are used. One tends to totally override the other.

When they're ready to talk, remind them of your parental duty and right to make decisions that affect their health, development and wellbeing, and accept that they do not agree or see the value in the choice you have made. Point out to them that you are not going to change your mind no matter what, and that you are not asking them to agree with you or to think the decision is a fair one. All you are asking is that they do as requested and desist from any unacceptable behaviour they may have exhibited.

Let them know that you love them and that they have a tremendous and admirable strength of character that you are proud of, but that they sometimes waste it on things they cannot change. Let them know that being someone with a passionate and stubborn nature is a good thing when used to fight for the right things. Ask them to consider whether this thing is really worth so much effort (effort that could go into other things), when it is not up for negotiation anyway. Let them know that they are missed within the family and would be welcomed back whenever they are ready to return.

Questions and answers

Q. *My ten-year-old son refuses to go to bed when I tell him to. He is adamant that it is his life and only he can say when he is tired. But if he stays up late, I find him difficult to get up* *in the morning. I also get very little downtime without him around.*

A. As you know, children need sleep to grow and they will need it even more as they move into adolescence, as this is when a lot of the brain restructuring that will turn them from a child into an adult takes place.

While you cannot make your child sleep, you *can* insist on a time when they are to be in bed every night. As he is ten, perhaps allow a later time for Friday and Saturday nights or other non-school nights, but these should still be set down.

Explain to him that you are aware that he may not sleep, but that he will definitely not sleep if he stays up. Let him know that his bedtime will get later as a matter of course as he gets older (perhaps with each birthday?).

Remind him that it is your responsibility to keep him as healthy as possible and that is why you are making this choice on his behalf, regardless of whether he feels it to be justified or not.

Negotiate with him a 'settling-down' period – perhaps ten or fifteen minutes between him going up to bed and you coming up to say goodnight, at which point he is expected to be in bed, washed with teeth brushed.

If you think it appropriate, you might allow him another half-hour on top of this to read before 'lights out'.

Many children today have televisions or games consoles in their room and will expect to play on them whenever they wish. Make it a trust arrangement between you that he does not use these after his bedtime, with the understanding that if he does, they will be taken out of his room for two weeks. Make this clear, so that he can't argue 'unfair' should you then take them away.

When he complies with the bedtime arrangements, make a big thing of it – praise his maturity and sensible behaviour.

Q. *Why is that kids always pick the worst time to throw a tantrum? My daughter, who entirely fits the profile for a B&C child, will always raise difficult issues when we are out shopping. Then, if I don't agree to what she wants, she throws a complete fit and I am so embarrassed in front of so many other people.*

A. Your child, like most B&C children, has learnt what works with you. The reason it always seems to happen at the worst possible moment is because she is smart enough to have worked out exactly when the worst moment for you is and to use your social embarrassment to her advantage.

There are a couple of options, but unfortunately neither of them involves her behaving differently – at first, anyway. However, by you changing your response to her strategy she will, in time, change her behaviour. No one as bright as a B&C wastes time on a certain losing hand.

Your can either:

   a) not give in to her, no matter what she says or does
or
   b) immediately remove yourself and her from the
      situation, until she is reasonable.

Both will be difficult and both will require you to make sacrifices. But the thing to remember is that whatever you may *think* is going on in other people's minds, you cannot possibly know it. You might be surprised at how supportive other people are feeling when your child behaves badly in a supermarket – they've all been there. You might also be surprised if you knew that the majority of people seeing you stick to your guns when your child behaves appallingly will see exactly what is happening and be fully on your side.

The second choice involves you dropping everything – literally – and walking out. This is dramatic and may well shock her the first time you do it. Drop your basket, or walk away from your trolley, then call her and walk out – don't wait for her, just march out. She'll try and get you to stop but don't let her do it. Be determined and let her know that you are. Once outside, you can either go home (very shocking and probably terribly inconvenient) or stand and have it out there and then.

Let her know that you are not prepared to be in a shop among other people with her behaving the way she was and drawing attention to you both that you are uncomfortable with. Let her know that whatever you have said 'No' to is an absolute 'No' and that it is not up for negotiation or challenge. You understand that she does not like it or agree with it and that is her right. However, you, as a parent, have to make decisions based on what is best, not only for her, but for yourself and other family members, and that is what you are doing.

If she is then prepared to behave in a more acceptable manner, resume the shopping (or start again if they've cleared the basket away).

Do not then try to appease your daughter by giving her something nice that you wouldn't normally buy. Otherwise you are rewarding her bad behaviour in another way and she will still be getting positive payback.

If she wants to pout or sulk her way round the shop, let her. You are not trying to control, only to manage behaviour appropriately. Nor does she have to agree with you or see your side of the argument. She may think you are being unfair but in B&C speak 'unfair' means 'not letting me have my way'.

Q. *I feel undermined by my partner. If I try to insist on something I think important, he will always say, 'Oh, go on, let him.' I know this is, in part, because he is not my son's* *father, but I find it difficult to be firm on an issue that is so unsupported.*

A. If this is happening when the two of you are alone discussing issues, then that is one thing. If this is happening in front of your son, then it is quite another. Discussion is fine; undermining your authority simply to score some popularity points with the boy is not.

If your partner feels so insecure about his place in your son's life, some serious talking as a family is in order about how you love and care for each other and, maybe, show it. One way he can show his love and care for both you and your son is to back you up in public, even if he wants to talk about it later in private. You, in return, will do the same with him as things arise.

Q. *Our children have a babysitter who does not stick to my rules when I am out. I regularly find they have stayed up later than intended, or been given things to eat that I would not choose. When I question the babysitter about what's going on, she just says my daughter told her it was OK. How can I insist on my boundaries being maintained when I am not there?*

A. Here are two suggestions:

1. Make sure you are leaving your children with a babysitter who is tough enough for them! If you have one or more B&C children make sure the babysitter understands the way they operate and the need to be firm. Don't just leave them with anyone 'nice'. They need a bit more than that.
2. Write a list of basic instructions that can be left with any babysitter and which includes:

    *   bedtimes
    *   programmes they are not allowed to watch – if any

- snacks or food they are allowed and options/quantities
- activities they may not do unsupervised
- equipment they are not allowed to touch
- games and activities they enjoy
- details of their routine (reading time before lights out, teeth cleaning, bath or showers, etc.)

You can involve the child or children in making the list and put in some extra information about the children that they can write themselves if they want.

5

'WHEN YOU'RE SMILING . . .'

Self-Esteem and the Art of Being Happy

CHAPTER SNAPSHOT

This chapter will focus on how the B&C child feels about themselves, and, in particular, on how and when they feel *good* about themselves.

A big risk with the B&C child is that you end up *not* dealing with situations that arise from their behaviour because you are worried that if their mood changes and they are upset, they will, in turn, take it out on other people and derail the equilibrium at home. The child can become a mini tyrant – controlling everyone through their temper and mood swings.

So, this chapter will look at self-esteem and then at happiness: what it is and what makes for a happy family. Every parent tends to claim that what they want is happy children (although as their children get older they tend to want happiness in combination with success), but in order to promote this, we need to understand happiness ourselves.

Happiness and the B&C child

When the B&C child is happy, the world is a good place for
all: the sun shines, they can be great company and are often
amusing and witty beyond their years. They provide everyone with entertainment and kindness – as long as it's on their
terms.

It is only to be expected that we all want to prolong the
times that are easy and happy and reduce those that are full
of conflict and painful emotions, so we tend to try to
appease the B&C child, to keep them happy and not tell
them things that might disturb their mood.

Over time, this means that they are treated differently
from other siblings or family members, and eventually they
may even become the controller of the family's mood. Don't
assume that the child is unaware of their powerful position.
Even very young children know which family member gets
their own way most often. In most families it will be Mum
or Dad or another key adult; in others it will be one particular child.

Siblings may also see the way in which the bad behaviour
or temper of one child leads them to get different treatment,
and they may begin to copy certain behavioural traits.
Younger siblings in particular can learn to copy B&C behaviour, even though they may not themselves meet the criteria
we use to identify a B&C child. They see it works and want
some of the associated attention.

Why do we treat B&C children differently?

Sometimes, you may let a child have their own way
because it's too much hassle to insist on changes, or because
you are eager (whether consciously or unconsciously) not

to be a target of the unkindness they display when provoked.

Sometimes, you may feel that showing them endless tolerance and compassion will teach them to be tolerant and compassionate in return. This is certainly true of children in general, as all these behaviours are learnt. However, most behaviour is adopted by an individual in order to get some kind of payback, or resulting effect. For the child who learns to be tolerant and kind, their behaviour gets them liked and smiled at; for the child who chooses to demand and tantrum, their behaviour gets them what they want as soon as they ask for it.

The angry B&C child's spite and venom can last for a long time, and if they are roused into real nastiness, the repercussions can go on for weeks – and no one wants to risk that. The child is also particularly powerful when a family occasion is looming. The threat that their mood or behaviour might ruin the family holiday or other long-awaited event is enough to make many parents go out of their way to appease or even bribe their child.

Parents can also be particularly vulnerable to a child who plays on their feelings of insecurity or guilt by criticising their parenting skills.

Whatever the reason, the end result can be that their bad behaviour is not consistently challenged. And when this happens it provides our child with the loophole they need – the possibility that if they play it right they can have things all their own way.

The long-term consequences of placating and giving in

Many people use the adjective 'arrogant' when describing older B&C children and assume that they have an over-developed sense of their own importance in relation to others. One of the reasons they seem this way is that they are used to being treated as very important and powerful people; their intelligence means that they have understood the reasons for this, and they become inclined to manipulate others, using the same tactics that they used as small children.

Ironically, the B&C child's sense of self or self-esteem is frequently much *less* robust than other children's. They have been continually boosted by being given in to, but that means they have not developed coping strategies for when things go wrong – and can remain quite fragile when things do not go their way. One of the ways in which this shows itself is by having little sense of humour when they themselves are at the centre of the joke. They cannot laugh at themselves easily or at their own shortcomings. They feel uncomfortable when their feelings are marginalised, and don't know how to cope with disappointment.

The B&C child lacks resilience. They do not take every-day social interaction well unless they are in an important role within it. It is common for them to blame everyone around them for the kind of actions that they themselves constantly exhibit. They may accuse others of bullying, for example, when they themselves are constantly teasing or name-calling. When a B&C child makes a mistake they may blame someone else for not correcting them. As they grow older, their parents will often take the brunt of much of this blame. 'It's all your fault' becomes a common refrain.

Resilience, like so much else in life, is learnt. Children need to learn that the boundaries of acceptable behaviour are, to some extent, universal; they are not dependent on the degree of distress or hurt caused to an individual, but rather the intention of the perpetrator. Some children do not truly understand that an action can be wrong even if the person on the receiving end of that action is not particularly distressed by it. An example of this would be name-calling. The child who calls their sibling 'a snivelling little rat' may decide they have done nothing wrong if that sibling laughs or walks away. If admonished they may well become indignant, insisting that no harm was done. They are unable to see that an act can be inherently wrong or unkind and that choosing to do it is therefore wrong or unkind. The same child may well become deeply distressed by their sibling ignoring them and demand that the sibling is punished. They are unable to distinguish between their own feelings of distress and the severity of the act of another.

Their parenting up to this point has often not helped; in being kept happy and away from confrontation, they are not getting any practice in dealing with their own feelings or understanding how others feel.

So, in the longer term, allowing the B&C child to continue to dominate the family mood is neither in their best interests, nor those of the family and siblings you are trying to protect. All this tiptoeing around them does nothing to promote intimacy at home; everyone is learning to hide their true feelings in order to keep the peace rather than using the safety of the family as a place to learn about personal boundaries, cause and effect.

Furthermore, if the B&C child is always placated – or allowed to make decisions that impact on everyone – they begin to believe that they are better at making those decisions than anyone else. They may export that behaviour to wider settings like school, where, if they try out similar behaviour with friends or other adults, they may end up feeling isolated and left out – but still believing the fault to lie firmly with everyone else.

Example

At ten-year-old Tom's school there is a policy that states that if a child cannot complete their homework, a parent sends in a note to the teacher outlining the reason. When this is done, no action is taken against the child for not having done their homework.

One Monday morning, Tom presents his teacher with a note, in his own handwriting and signed by him, saying that he has been unable to complete his homework as he spent the weekend at his cousin's house. The teacher kindly but firmly tells him that this is not acceptable, and that the letter has to come from a parent. Tom responds angrily that the teacher is being unfair as both his parents are very busy people and that he is perfectly capable of telling her the reason why he could not complete his homework – or is she implying that he is lying?

The B&C child can seem so mature and grown-up in their language and behaviour. But in reality they are a child like any other, only they are desperate for attention and equate that attention with how much they are loved, valued and wanted. The more people notice them, the more they can tell that they stand out in the eyes of others, and the more they feel good about themselves.

Their family circumstances have taught them what they need to do to get their own way: be it bullying, being eloquent or witty and charming. For most such children, it is a volatile mixture of all of these. This is their tried-and-tested means to an end.

The bottom line is that they are not self-sufficient. Like everyone else's, the B&C child's feelings alter in response to the feedback of others. But unlike everybody else, they are not interested in the words you use or the emotions you express, only in how large they are in your eyes – and how important you appear to find them.

Self-esteem

There are two fundamentally different ways in which we may see ourselves.

This first relies on a degree of self-knowledge. It means we see who we are, how we are and what we are (and are not) good at, but we attach no greater worth to any one feature of ourselves than to the others (although we may prefer some): 'I am a unique and special recipe – there is no one in the world quite like me.'

This way of seeing ourselves is based on an understanding that while we have many component parts, for most of us no one feature of our being is unique and outstanding on its own. We are all made up of the same ingredients. So just as you can take flour, milk, eggs, butter and sugar and create any number of different cakes, pancakes, biscuits, scones or pastries, so the various human ingredients can be mixed together to make an infinite number of different human beings. It is the mixture of features and elements that gives us value and individuality, making us unique. So while one person may well be better at something than another, it does not mean that overall they are of more value or worth as a person. One person may have invented a vaccine that has saved millions of lives, and while this may mean that they have made a greater contribution to the wellbeing of others than most other people around them, it still does not mean that they are a better or more valuable person, only that their actions in a certain area have been more valuable.

We all have potential, and children need to learn that what they do can change the way people see them for better or worse, but who they are is neither more nor less valuable than any other person.

The second way of seeing ourselves (shown in the linear

model on p. 99) is quite different. In this model, each person has their place in a group hierarchy, and the group could be a family, a class at school, a collection of friends, a business or a club.

The individual's place within the group defines their worth. Those at the top are more important and therefore 'better' than those at the bottom. This way of seeing people in relation to each other is the thought process that supports various forms of prejudice such as racism (assumes people to have places in the pecking order according to race with a clear hierarchy of value) or sexism (believes that everything pertaining to one sex is superior and of more value than anything that typifies the other).

Most children have a sense of hierarchy (as do we all) and can easily say who is best at maths or who can run fastest. However, most children do accept that this indicates the value of their skills, not their value as a person. B&C children frequently have an overdeveloped sense of hierarchy and truly believe that those at the top of the list are of more worth than those who are in the middle or at the bottom.

The motivation derived from the hierarchical model can vary. People who view the world in this way are often motivated to succeed by the belief that if they work hard they can climb the ladder and reach the top. However, for those who see themselves below the halfway line, motivation may be poor and they may feel like a failure and simply give up trying.

It's also interesting to note that children who bully have often got an overdeveloped sense of hierarchy. They too see everyone's value as related to their place in the perceived order. This allows them to treat those they consider below them as they please, and encourages attempts to 'bring down a peg or two' those just above, in order to allow them to progress a little higher up themselves.

Two Models of Self-Esteem

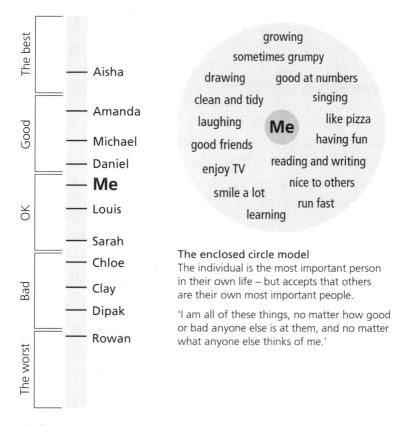

The best

Good

OK

Bad

The worst

— Aisha

— Amanda

— Michael

— Daniel

— **Me**

— Louis

— Sarah

— Chloe

— Clay

— Dipak

— Rowan

growing

sometimes grumpy

drawing   good at numbers

clean and tidy   singing

laughing   **Me**   like pizza

good friends   having fun

enjoy TV   reading and writing

   nice to others

smile a lot

   run fast

learning

The enclosed circle model
The individual is the most important person
in their own life – but accepts that others
are their own most important people.

'I am all of these things, no matter how good
or bad anyone else is at them, and no matter
what anyone else thinks of me.'

The linear model
This model only allows an individual to feel good about themselves by
comparing themselves favourably with others. It divides everything up –
everyone can't be equally good, there has to be hierarchy. Someone has
to be the best – and therefore someone has to be the worst.

This is not to suggest that all B&C children are bullies, or
vice versa, but it is undoubtedly true that such children do
on occasion bully others through their demands and behaviour. The difference is usually that while the B&C child

simply sees it as a case of exercising their rights to behave how they like, the bullying child has the *intention* of lowering the self-worth of others through their actions. The outcome for those on the receiving end may well be the same.

Example

At twelve years old Lottie was a very bright girl from a very competitive family, who, as expected, won a place at a girls' grammar school – a hugely prestigious achievement within the local area. Once there, she found it difficult because having always effortlessly been top in her primary school, she was now surrounded by other very bright children and really had to struggle to maintain a position. At the end of her second year, she decided to drop chemistry, even though she wanted to be a doctor, because she was given a 'B' in her end-of-term assessment rather than the 'A' she was expecting. Now, aged twenty-five, and a qualified accountant, she has always rather regretted not doing medicine.

Helping your child

The B&C child needs help in forming a more holistic view of themselves; to see themselves as a person capable of good and bad, highs and lows, great acts and foolish ones. At the moment, they will probably have considerable trouble accepting half of these. To the B&C child, only the extremes count, although many will be quite comfortable accepting themselves as people who are capable of extreme naughtiness or wild behaviour – particularly if these things have kudos within their peer group or draw great attention within their family. The characteristics that they'll find hardest to own are those that they see as undesirable or unsuccessful.

If you can help them see themselves more fully, they will hopefully become less attention-seeking. Just as most children grow out of the attention-driven stages of childhood as they mature, so helping the child to overcome their self-worth issues can help them to mature and grow too.

Having said that, you'll have to acknowledge that older children may well have got into the habit of behaving in certain ways all the time, and that such habits can be hard to break – even if the underlying reasons for the behaviour have shifted. Many B&C children will be used to dominating every situation and putting down any attempt at power-sharing by the time they are seven or eight – so to change at ten may well take time and patience.

When dealing with the behaviour of the B&C child you need to ensure that you avoid, whenever possible, putting them down in public as this tends to humiliate them. Comparing the child unfavourably with others or with siblings is also not a good idea as the angry child may well take out their frustrations and hurt on that other child or sibling.

And a final word on hierarchies: while moving a B&C child towards a more holistic view of themselves, it's important not to try and undermine their current feeling of 'place' within a hierarchy. So it's not a good plan to tell them repeatedly that the things they are using to justify their position don't matter – because to them they do. You're trying to help them to see themselves in a more rounded way and to accept that others may feel in a similar way about themselves too.

Example

Amy, a new girl, has joined the class, and she is rapidly assumed to be both cleverer and prettier than eight-year-old-Gala – the previous title holder.

Gala is distraught and declares that she will not go to school any more. She refuses to discuss what is wrong and simply says that the new girl is 'picking on' her and that she hates her. Amy is willing to be friends but is getting upset by Gala's unkindness and manipulative behaviour.

The teacher takes Gala aside. She asks for her help in settling Amy into the class, as she can see that there are problems with the girls accepting her, and that the only person clever and skilful enough to sort it out fairly and kindly is her. She then sets up a time at lunchtime when Gala is allowed to come and see the teacher in the library (when no one else is allowed in the building) to give her a progress report. Every day when Gala gives her report the teacher reinforces how clever and capable Gala is, and how well she is looking after Amy.

The importance of empathy

All children need help to develop empathy – the ability to put themselves in others' shoes. B&C children need even more help with this as they tend to be preoccupied with themselves and have little understanding of their own emotional self, let alone the emotions of others and how these might affect them. Children learn to empathise at different speeds; some will never learn to do it entirely – and it is probably true that no one is capable of fully empathising with others while experiencing anger or other overwhelming emotions. However, you can help your child to develop – as far as they are able – by asking them to work out what a person in a particular situation may be feeling. Stories in the media and television soaps offer an excellent opportunity for doing this. If your child can come up with an answer, and think about how someone else may be feeling, praise them for their insight. This will encourage them to use insight again, the next time a similar situation arises.

**TOP TIPS FOR ENCOURAGING THE
DEVELOPMENT OF SELF-ESTEEM IN A BRIGHT
AND CHALLENGING CHILD**

• Self-esteem is developed through a sense of achievement. Encourage your child to reflect on their achievements regularly – perhaps 'three things I have achieved today' for each member of the family at an evening meal or bedtime.

• Set a positive example by expressing your own sense of accomplishment. Many of us worry that saying how well we have done something is boasting – it's not; boasting is when we use our own accomplishments to put someone else down. Just owning them is good for your self-esteem. So get used to saying out loud, within your child's earshot, 'I'm proud of myself. Someone was really rude to me in the supermarket today, and I didn't get angry. I just told them that I thought they were being rude and they apologised.'

• Encourage their achievements to be non-competitive – such as helping others, obeying you without arguing, being kind and thoughtful, tidying their room without being asked and so on. If they suggest competitive achievements, by all means applaud them, but let them know that you are looking to share things that show them to be a rounded and kind person, not just how clever they are. If they don't understand the difference, let them learn by example, as everyone shares.

• You might have targets that you set with your child in relation to their behaviour and issues that regularly cause friction, such as going to bed on time without a fuss. If they are working towards such a target, set up a record sheet or star chart for them. Don't offer a material reward as the end result – rather use their competitive streak (most B&C children have one) to see if they can get an agreed number of stars in a row.

- Encourage them to notice how it feels to be getting it right/doing what they've been asked to do and receiving positive feedback.
- Give plenty of praise and attention at all times – and to their efforts as a whole rather than the end results.
- Talk to them about others in terms of their broader qualities, not just their outstandingly successful areas. So if your child idolises a footballer or a TV star, ask them about what kind of a person they are, not just about their football skills or looks. The modern cult of celebrity teaches children the opposite – that an outstanding ability means you are an outstanding person. This is generally not true.
- Encourage them to keep a folder or box in which they can put things to remind them of key events. Photos from outings, cinema ticket stubs, programmes or fliers of events they've attended, letters or postcards they've received or even sent themselves. Once a year, perhaps on their birthday, sit with them and select items to stick into a yearbook – a reminder of things that happened. Spend time reflecting on the good things they have done and events they have enjoyed.
- Every time they use the words 'I can't', make them say three sentences beginning with 'I can'. Make a game of it. You'll probably have to do it too!

What makes people happy?

REFLECTION EXERCISE

Read through the quotations below and decide on the three that most sum up happiness for you.

Happiness is when what you think, what you say, and what you do are in harmony.

Mohandas K. Gandhi

The Grand essentials of happiness are: something to do, something to love, and something to hope for.

Allan K. Chalmers

You will never be happy if you continue to search for what happiness consists of. You will never live if you are looking for the meaning of life.

Albert Camus

Success is not the key to happiness. Happiness is the key to success. If you love what you are doing, you will be successful.

Albert Schweitzer

Happiness belongs to the self-sufficient.

Aristotle

The happiness that is genuinely satisfying is accompanied by the fullest exercise of our faculties and the fullest realisation of the world in which we live.

Bertrand Russell

Happiness comes when your work and words are of benefit to yourself and others.

Buddha

❝There are as many nights as days, and the one is just as long as the other in the year's course. Even a happy life cannot be without a measure of darkness, and the word "happy" would lose its meaning if it were not balanced by sadness.❞

Carl Jung

❝If only we'd stop trying to be happy we'd have a pretty good time.❞

Edith Wharton

❝Unhappiness is best defined as the difference between our talents and our expectations.❞

Edward de Bono

❝You can never get enough of what you don't need to make you happy.❞

Eric Hoffer

❝The true way to render ourselves happy is to love our work and find in it our pleasure.❞

Françoise de Motteville

❝There is only one happiness in life, to love and be loved.❞

George Sand

❝Many people have a wrong idea of what constitutes true happiness. It is not attained through self-gratification, but through fidelity to a worthy purpose.❞

Helen Keller

❝That is happiness; to be dissolved into something completely great.❞

Willa Cather

Feedback

Now look at the three quotes you have chosen:

- Are they all similar?
- In what ways?
- What does this say about you?

Try this exercise with your partner or your child if they are old enough to understand – it might tell you a lot about each other.

Many people are quite surprised when they try this exercise that the quotes they have chosen seem to fit well together even if they are not identical in character. When asked, many of us find it hard to define what happiness is, but when looking at the words of others it is often clear that happiness lies in helping or doing things for others and trying to benefit the world with our thoughts, words and actions.

The quotes in the exercise are quite complex for many children, but when parents asked their children what made them most happy or when did they feel most happy (as opposed to excited) they frequently replied that it was when they were engaged in activities they enjoyed, felt capable or good at and which had set expectations or rules attached. There were also many examples where children were happiest when not being too conscious of themselves – when they were swept up in the moment by an activity, such as football, dancing, singing or reading.

Much has been written about happiness. Many people have tried and failed to find its true nature; others don't analyse but seem to have it in abundance. Is being able to experience true happiness about the chemicals in our brains or just being able to identify what will make us happy?

So often what we think will make us happy only serves to make us want something else the moment we get it. Material things never make anyone happy for long – a new model comes along, boredom and complacency set in or fashion changes. Teaching children to reflect on how things make them feel will help them learn what makes them happy in the truest sense, as opposed to the fleeting and transient happiness that getting what they want when they want it provides.

By and large, it seems that what genuinely makes us happy contains all or some of the following:

- focusing on other people
- not being self-obsessed
- spotting the moment
- learning to feel joy
- a sense of connectedness to the world as a whole and taking pleasure in being
- saying pleasant things
- staying conscious of good things
- being part of a loving relationship (friendship, family, lover, parent/child)
- being absorbed in what we are doing

We need to help all children learn to be happy – recent surveys have shown that young people in the UK are the least happy in Europe, despite (or perhaps because of) their material advantages. But for the B&C child happiness can be even more elusive, as they find almost all the things on the above list difficult. This inability to feel happy may well put the B&C child at risk as an adult of the behaviours that people who cannot experience happiness fall into – alcohol and drug abuse, casual sex, extreme risk behaviour and thrill-seeking, to name but a few.

REFLECTION EXERCISE

Can you think of ten things that make you/have made you truly happy for a moment or two? They should be simple everyday things – here's our list to give you a sample:

- flying a kite
- paddling in a warm sea
- feeling the warmth of the sun on our faces
- seeing a rainbow
- holding hands with someone we love
- feeling the wind whipping around us when we're wrapped up warmly
- holding a sleeping child
- standing at the top of a steep hill after climbing it
- riding a bike with a friend in flip-flops with the sun on our backs
- wading through a field of long grass leaving tracks

Perhaps you might ask your child for their top ten too – it might tell you a lot about what they feel happiness is all about. For us it's all about being in the moment and being in the world.

And all the time I was thinking: *This*. It was the feeling of being consumed completely by the moment. Being in the centre of my own time. Knowing that all the while I was loitering about upon this old world . . . I had this moment now . . . Like a bead, the present, the awareness of it. Like a bead on a string that I might have pressed into my palm as I slid off towards death . . . *This*.'

Kirsty Gunn, *44 Things: A Year of Life at Home*

What makes a B&C child happy?

First and foremost being the centre of attention. We might believe that they only want to be the centre of good attention but, in fact, if the option is between being the centre of negative attention (a row or telling-off, for example) or no attention, most opt for the attention every time. This may be quite different from how you are, or how you were at their age, so it can be hard to understand. For most B&C children, this is the most important characteristic of their personality, closely followed by their need to win.

It follows that negative feedback to the B&C child should always be voiced as 'constructive criticism' – pointing out how they might improve rather than harping on about their shortcomings. Where possible, a target built into the process of change will appeal to their competitive streak, and may help them take up the challenge to change. For example, 'I would really appreciate it if you would take your empty plate into the kitchen after you have had a snack, as I'm always tripping over the debris by the sofa. For every plate you take out, draw a smiley face on the chart on the fridge and if there are more than ten by the weekend, you can choose the movie for us all to watch on Saturday night.'

If an issue arises where their behaviour has caused conflict or upset, they must be helped to take responsibility for their actions without necessarily feeling blamed. When they feel unduly criticised they will not accept responsibility at all.

Example

What *not* to do: 'Now you've done it! Daniel is upstairs crying his eyes out, Lauren is sulking in the garden and I'm here yet again on a Sunday having to talk to you about your behaviour. Why can't you just get on for a couple of hours?

Is it so hard to let your brother and sister play too? I'm so fed up with you; this family would be fine if only you'd stop winding everyone up all the time.'

The clever approach: 'Oh dear – we seem to have a situation here. Everyone seems to be upset with everyone else. I wonder what happened? [Then, to your B&C child:] You're the most sensible when it comes to telling a tale so what happened?'

As they talk about what everyone else did, listen intently and ask kindly, 'What did you do?' or, 'What did you say?' If they give any information about their own involvement praise them for their honesty and ask another question. If they still refuse to give any information about themselves, it may be that in the past they have felt judged and blamed by you, in which case you should let them realise you won't do that again.

Or you may have to reassure them, 'I'm not going to get angry with you, I just want to understand what happened, and as you're usually honest, I thought I'd ask you first.'

It may help to give them some 'get outs' too such as, 'I know Daniel can be annoying when he talks in that silly voice, it sometimes annoys me too.' This may encourage them to tell you more about what set them off if they feel you empathise with their viewpoint.

How to help B&C children to be happy

Encourage your child to reflect on how they feel in certain settings. When you go out and about, ask them to notice beauty and life around them. Gill has a friend who when they walk together asks, 'What was your best childhood memory?' or, 'What was the best cake you ever ate?' Gill's favourite was when they were walking in Kew Gardens and her friend asked her, 'Which is your favourite tree?'

Noticing the world around you, noticing your own responses to it and noticing others' helps you to be happy. So you must encourage children to do just this. You can do so by recording your experiences through photo albums, scrapbooks, blogs, collections, putting things into special boxes, framing things they may value and putting them on the wall. Most of all you can notice and express your responses by talking about them and sharing how you feel.

Example

Ten-year-old Fergus, the youngest of four children with strong B&C tendencies, likes tidiness and dislikes clutter. In his need to clear things out, he often ends up throwing things away that he could reflect upon to make him see that he is valued. His mother, who is in the habit of squirrelling away some of his things, finds his 'Circle time' chart from school about why he is special. She sticks it in a frame, so that everyone can see what his classmates thought of him. He is quite pleased.

Encourage your child to give praise to others and to give themselves a pat on the back for doing it. You may have to model the process, so they see what to do. For example, at mealtimes ask everyone in turn to state:

- the highlight of the year so far, or
- one way they were helpful today, or
- two things someone said that showed them they were liked, or
- something about themselves that they feel proud of

You might also try some other ways to let them feel loved and valued, such as:

- leaving them little notes when they did things well ('Post-it' notes are great for this)
- encouraging them to do kind and thoughtful things back – buying them their own pack of Post-its
- giving little presents that show you love them; nothing enormous – perhaps a new pair of socks – just something to show you were thinking of them
- drawing them a cartoon referring to something they will understand
- giving a treat in relation to their good behaviour/kindness, etc.
- giving lots of praise and feedback when they offer a reflection on how others must be feeling
- finding them a useful and positive role when other people are the centre of attention (e.g. helping at a family party) – rather than excluding them
- being generous in encouraging positive reflection on others and picking up themes (*without* constantly going back over things they told you about others and asking for an update, which, in our experience, always means they wish they had not told you in the first place)

Questions and answers

Q. *My twelve-year-old son's birthday party is coming up and he is adamant that he does not want his ten-year-old brother to attend. He wants a small party, with just a few friends invited. Should I be adamant that his brother is allowed to attend – because he is his brother – although also insist that he behaves well? Or should I take him away for the day, so he is not there to 'spoil' the party at all?*

A. Rather than giving him a treat on what should be his brother's day (by taking him out instead), why not make him part of the organisation? Encourage him to think about what would really make his elder brother's day, perhaps by talking to his friends, and then get him to explore possible options – where the best pizza comes from, suggestions as to what kind of video they would like to watch, where everyone could sleep if a sleepover is planned and how he could help at the party (e.g. pour the drinks or cook the food). Could he make decorations, buy the party plates, blow up balloons, etc.? Or could he have a T-shirt with 'staff' written on it and try to be a waiter?

Q. *If I try to tell my B&C child about something I am not happy with, rather than accept it he tends to sulk, which, because no one enjoys it, I try to avoid. How can I get him to listen to me because the changes I want to make are for his own good?*
A. You can't directly change his behaviour (you have already tried and it does not work) but you can change yours and hope he changes his to match.

Try asking him to make a specific change in the future rather than criticising his behaviour in the past. You might also set up a simple reward or feedback system for when he manages to do it differently.

Q. *If something goes wrong for my B&C child he tends to produce an overdramatic reaction, saying that he knows how awful he is, and he wishes he was dead. This scares me. I worry that he is at risk of self-harming – or even worse.*
A. Encourage him to see himself not just in terms of absolutes (good/bad; fat/thin; ugly/beautiful) but in a more holistic way. Help him to deal with uncomfortable feelings that come from knock-backs – everyone has them. No, it

does not feel good right now, but life gets better, and sharing feelings helps. At some level this is attention-grabbing behaviour. He is letting you know how extreme his feelings are and making a statement that will affect you – perhaps even encourage you to go out of your way to 'fix' his feelings for him by giving him a treat, perhaps. If this has happened in the past you must make sure it doesn't happen again.

Comfort him that by explaining that everyone feels bad when things go wrong, but that time does help. Tomorrow or the next day he will have moved on from the painful feelings.

To reassure you here – the fact that he is saying these things probably means he is unlikely to self-harm. Most self-harmers keep their self-destructive feelings secret from others; either because they have to or because they don't know how to do it any differently. It's part of the behaviour.

Q. *My nine-year-old daughter regularly gives her five-year-old sister a really hard time. They share a bedroom and she is adamant that her sister should not cross over into her half (she has put a line down the middle) or touch any of her 'stuff'. She won't let her have friends to play and by insisting on her rights at all times, she is taking away her sister's. How do I get her to share and be kinder?*

A. It looks like she is being territorial because she feels threatened, so make time just to spend with her, so she realises she is valued. Then, when your younger daughter has friends around to play, perhaps she can have a special time somewhere else, say with you, watching television – a 'treat' for being so kind to her sister.

Give her lots of positive feedback about when she is helpful and kind; take her shopping and get her to do the trolley loading or let her help you unload it if it is delivered. Make her see that she is valued.

This should help her see (albeit probably unconsciously) that she doesn't have to exert her authority and existence at home. In other words, don't deal with the behaviour she is exhibiting but look at the emotional needs that are prompting it – helping her to meet them elsewhere.

6

WHERE THE BUCK STOPS

Encouraging Personal Responsibility

CHAPTER SNAPSHOT

In this chapter we'll be exploring the balance needed in life between personal expression and social acceptability – the conflict between 'being me' and the impact my behaviour has on everyone else.

This is something we all struggle with, to some extent. For B&C children, however, the bit about 'being themselves' tends to prevail over any appreciation of how their behaviour impacts on other people.

So, for harmony in the family now, and to help them build better relationships with other people in the future, they must learn how to recognise the rights and values of other people, and how to live with them.

What is personal responsibility?

Today, the concept of personal responsibility has become rather unfashionable and dated to many. It involves seeing ourselves as the instigator and originator of the consequences that result from our actions and choices. These days, it's far more common to look for someone else to blame for every-thing that happens, rather than to accept the responsibility for our own actions and behaviours. For example, fast-food companies have been sued by overweight people for produ-cing fattening food, cigarette companies by people with lung cancer and the producers of computer games by parents whose children are violent. While we are not condoning making money from fast food, cigarettes or violent computer games, we wonder at which point the consumer takes respon-sibility for their own choices?

On an individual level, children and young people have always found admitting their mistakes tough, but it seems to have become almost impossible for anyone to accept another's views without having to 'win' and have the last word. Criticising others has always been common but it has reached epidemic proportions, no doubt fed by reality TV, paparazzi and gossip magazines letting us into others' lives in an unparalleled way. But while criticism of others has never seemed as acceptable or overt as it is now, self-review and taking responsibility have never been so little in evi-dence.

While we are not responsible for the behaviour of others – they choose that for themselves – we must take some respon-sibility for setting up situations where people are likely to behave in certain ways. So if you say something critical to someone in a sharp way they may well respond rudely. You are not responsible for their rudeness – that is their choice – but you are responsible for speaking in such a way that the person was likely to feel angry or upset.

It follows that the child who constantly 'winds up' a sib-ling and gets hit in return needs to understand the role they played in provoking the behaviour. Hitting a sibling is a wrong choice, but the behaviour that led to the choice was also wrong, and they have to some extent reaped what they sowed. Had they behaved differently, the outcome might also have been different.

We are generally better at identifying what others have done wrong to us than we are at identifying what we have done wrong to them. The verbally able B&C child is able to take a dispute back several days or weeks if need be, to show that they were simply reacting to the unacceptable and unfair behaviour of others. They are – in their own eyes – in no way to blame. They usually have good memories too, and can recall fine details that others may have forgotten. Their brightness may also lead them to embroider the truth a little, if not tell downright lies on occasion, and their ability to remember small details or to create them can often seem very convincing to someone who is relatively tongue-tied.

What is social responsibility?

Generally this is the way in which our behaviour impacts on others; how the choices we make detract from, restrict or enable the choices of others. So when someone chooses to have a long, loud and personal conversation on a mobile phone on a train about their love life, it takes away the right of others to their own thoughts and conversations by intruding into them. We live in a society that is very crowded and we need to understand that our choices create or reduce the stress, problems and options available to other people.

While we have the right to make our own choices we also have a responsibility to ensure that the choices we make for ourselves do not impinge upon the right of other individuals within our society to make their own choices. This is social responsibility.

Society is not a fixed thing and what is acceptable may change from group to group, country to country, year to year. Things we do today as standard would have shocked our great-grandparents. For example, eating in the street, having loud conversations, and showing emotion in public – whether anger, sadness or joy – would have formerly been considered very bad manners. Furthermore, new technology becomes available to all and this results in different behaviours. Even ten years ago mobile phones were nowhere near as commonly available as they are today, and their use is having an impact on how we walk along the street. And now that there are food and drink outlets everywhere, it's no wonder that behaviour in relation to eating and drinking in public has changed. However, while boundaries may shift and change with time, the right of the individual to personal space within society, both physical and emotional, remains fundamental. Everyone has equal right to be part of society without being intimidated; we all have to share space without some intruding on that (be it real or abstract) of others.

How do you learn personal and social responsibility?

Normally, this starts almost as soon as a child is aware of others around them. They are taught to behave in appropriate ways by being encouraged or restricted according to what they do and the circumstances around them. So the child pulling at Mum's clothes while she is talking to someone else learns that interrupting someone will get you nowhere; the child demanding a toy from another at a toddler group learns that they have to wait their turn; and the noisy three-year-old in the café is calmed, shushed and engaged by adults to keep their noise to an acceptable level.

However, in some cases a sense of personal responsibility does not develop as it should. Sometimes this is due to a parent simply giving in – giving the child attention when they demand it; letting the screaming child have the toy they want; or letting the child make as much noise as they like in a public place, while they simply shrug their shoulders help-lessly at the people around them. In other cases, it is not developing because the child has a problem with under-standing or coping with society, whether large or small. Such children would normally be considered to have special needs and may, for example, be on the autism spectrum, as well displaying other special characteristics.

Every child will learn differently and some need great patience and tolerance to get them to the same point that a sibling reached all by themselves. However, if this sense is not developing properly in a child, then they are not being socialised in the way that they should be.

Sometimes parents have difficulty in saying 'No' to their children, and find this particularly difficult when the reasons are abstract: 'because somebody might not like it' seems a feeble excuse, while, 'People have a right not to live with your choices' is too convoluted. They also sometimes strug-gle with where their own (and their child's) rights are in relation to others', and why one should take precedence over another. A mother recently told us that she had a problem finding any reason why her son should not play his music out loud in public because he had as much right to hear it as others did not to hear it.

Our answer to such issues is always to consider the larger number of people affected by an action as a rough guide to its suitability in a given situation. Unless you can canvas opinion and prove that the majority are in favour of your choice of action, assume that they are not.

B&C children are usually difficult to socialise well –

that's why they are challenging in the first place. Learning their place in the hierarchy of the family alone is problematic; as far as they are concerned, they are the most significant member of the family. Your job is not to try to diminish them by telling them that they are not, rather to reassure them that they are very important – but so is everyone else.

Children, like the rest of us, tend not to learn through words. Rather than having their behaviour rationally explained to them, they will learn through personal experience with some reflection afterwards. Behaving in ways that others don't like will bring its own knock-backs and the child will have to cope with being challenged for selfishness, bossiness or unkindness – whatever the situation leads to.

In the modern world of parenting and educating, there isn't enough opportunity for children to receive effective feedback from their peers without an adult stepping in to sort things out for them. But the moment an adult steps in, the situation becomes all about words and talking it through, which might mean leaving the important emotional content out altogether. Most adults feel they are doing the right thing by behaving this way. They feel they are teaching the child the 'grown-up' way of dealing with things unemotionally.

Instead, they are deskilling the child. They are making the natural impulse of the child to express things their own way unacceptable, expecting them to concentrate on words in ways they are not yet able to do. It's understandable – they don't want to see them hurt or harmed – but they are preventing real, child-friendly communication about what is and what is not acceptable to an individual and to wider society.

A small child who pushes another away is expressing in

their own way how unacceptable the contact or involvement of that child is to them at that moment. Adults often jump in, telling them to 'play nicely' and not to push. In this case, the child who is being pushed away has learnt nothing except that the child who pushed them is wrong or mean. Their own behaviour has not been questioned.

The correct approach is to say that pushing is unacceptable; but if you want him to leave you alone, *tell* him to leave you alone, and if you want him to go away, tell him to go away. Discourage the physical reaction, rather than trying to do away with the emotional expression – just make it more appropriate.

Similarly, there is a tendency to stop conflict between children of any age when it arises. But preventing them from sorting things out for themselves denies them the opportunity to develop strategies for learning reactions and how they impact on others. An invaluable learning process is prevented: how to adapt behaviour according to the reactions it causes.

It is challenging for adults to watch children upsetting each other. We certainly could not allow a child to physically hurt another without stepping in, particularly if the children are of different ages or temperaments. However, leaving them as much as possible to get on or fall out with each other is important.

We are finding that children in schools are seriously unskilled in 'getting on with others' because they have had too much supervision: constant structured care from a young age with other young people. It seems to have become a feature of modern parenting that a child is never left alone without adult supervision, the result being that many children are less able to cope with the argy-bargy of life because other people have always sorted out their problems. Even those children who are more used to getting involved in social interaction are having a hard time, because the 'over-adulted' children they mix with go running for help every time anything that they don't like is said or done. All children need to understand and manage the impact their behaviour has on other people.

So, try to find a way to let children interact with each other in their own way, and without you present, as much as possible. Leave them to play in the garden without watching over them, take them to a small enclosed park and let them free, while you stay in one place. However, bear in mind that leaving them to their own devices in an indoor public place, such as a café, is not a good idea. Gill recently went to a Starbucks one Sunday morning, and had a miserable time while seven or eight children ran, whooped, played rough and tumble and generally yelled their heads off while their parents completely ignored them. Hardly a lesson in socialisation or personal responsibility!

Example
A young person gets on to a train with their MP3 player in action (without headphones). The resulting noise impacts on everyone, but rather than understanding the effect their behaviour is having on others sharing the same space, when asked to turn it off the young person responds by saying: 'Where does it say I can't?'

The three questions technique

Most children will admit their mistakes when it is clear to them that they have made one. For some, it might take a fair bit of time and energy to get them to recognise them – but with the B&C child it can take for ever. While they may be gracious enough to admit minor errors, usually to draw attention to their goodness by doing so, they will almost never admit to serious ones.

But while getting the B&C child to take responsibility for their actions can be trying, it is vital that you do it. If allowed to get away with passing the buck or avoiding the consequences of their actions they will continue this behaviour into adulthood, which will make them difficult and unreasonable friends, colleagues and partners, and may lead to them being unpopular and isolated.

The one thing you don't do is to blame the child directly for any incident or event. If you ask them to admit they did anything wrong, they simply won't do it – or they will do it with bad grace, and only under pressure. When the B&C child feels blamed, someone else will bear the brunt of their feelings. They may retaliate against the person who has already been on the receiving end of their behaviour 'for getting them into trouble'; they may take it out on anyone near at hand; or they may take it out on you, by becoming hateful, spiteful and not co-operating for a long time.

You should find ways of helping the child recognise for themselves that their behaviour has had negative consequences for someone else and that they must make amends somehow.

The easiest way of doing this is by using the three questions technique as follows:

1. What did you do?
Keep repeating the question without being diverted until it is answered. If the child is bursting to tell you what someone else did just repeat 'I'm not asking what so and so did, I'm asking what did you do?'

This is about getting them to take responsibility for their own behaviour.

2. What should/could you have done?

'Should' is about getting them to acknowledge that they know the 'rules', either formal or informal, about behaviour.

'Could' is used if there are no apparent rules, it is about encouraging them to think about the choices they might have made.

3. What can you do now to put things right?

You don't have to accept the first suggestion. If the wrong-doing was against someone else they should be the one to accept or refuse the proffered solution wherever possible.

This has to be done in a calm and kind voice, no matter how you feel inside!

Example

Nine-year-old Rowan has just torn up her little sister Ruby's picture of a unicorn that she had stuck up on her bedroom wall. Ruby is five.

First off, Rowan tries to deny there has been a problem:

> MUM: Rowan, Ruby is crying. Has something happened?
> ROWAN: I don't know.
> MUM: I don't think that's the truth, Rowan. What did you do?

Rowan realises then that she cannot avoid the situation, so she tries to shift blame. Mum is kind and listens but is not diverted from the question:

> ROWAN: She called me bossy!
> MUM: Did she? That wasn't kind, but I asked what did you do?

Rowan now sees that she is backing herself into a corner, so she tries to lash out at Mum with a little emotional knife-turning:

ROWAN: She's always calling me names, and you always stick up for her not me.

MUM: I'm sorry you feel that way, Rowan, but I still want an answer – what did you do?

Rowan is now running out of places to go, so she starts to cry.

MUM: Rowan, there's no need to cry. I just want to know what you did. The quicker you answer me, the quicker we can put this all behind us and get on to doing something else.

ROWAN [shouts loudly]: I tore her stupid picture! There, are you happy now?

MUM [calmly]: Well done for telling the truth. I know it can be hard sometimes. Did you tear up her picture before or after she called you bossy?

ROWAN: After. She started it.

MUM: Well, I'll certainly talk to Ruby. It's not kind to call people names. What could you have done when Ruby called you bossy that wouldn't have made her cry?

ROWAN: She's a baby. She cries for nothing.

MUM: I think she's crying right now because you tore her picture. What could you have done differently, Rowan?

ROWAN: Told her to shut her big mouth!

MUM: What do you think she would have done then?

ROWAN: Don't know and don't care!

Mum gives Rowan a hug and says that she'll leave her alone in her room for five minutes to see if she can think of something she could have done differently so that Ruby would not have cried. She tells Rowan to come and find her when she's had an idea. Mum finishes by telling Rowan that she'll find a solution in no time because she's a very clever girl. After about fifteen minutes Rowan comes to find her. Mum greets her with a smile

> MUM: Hello, sweetheart, have you managed to think of something you could have done differently?
>
> ROWAN: Yes, I could have ignored her and gone to play in another room and then she would have realised how much I hate her and then she would have had to come and say sorry to me, or I wouldn't talk to her.
>
> MUM: I knew you'd think it through. You're so clever when you take the time to think. You're right. It was Ruby who should have been made to feel sorry, but you made a choice that left her feeling even more upset than you were. She got all the 'poor yous' instead of you. Now what will you do to make it up to your sister?
>
> ROWAN: She can choose one of my pictures. I've got lots.
>
> MUM: Good idea. When she's calmed down, I will have a word with her about calling you names, shall I?
>
> ROWAN: No, leave it for today. She'll only get upset again.
>
> MUM: How thoughtful of you. OK then.

Developing a sense of responsibility

1. Let children deal with things themselves and allow them to take the consequences of their actions, so they learn to understand cause and effect. Let them see that other people feel strongly without sanitising the experience.

B&C children can verbalise in a way that their peers can't – so allowing them to take the consequences of re-actions they have provoked is a good thing to do.

Example
During a game of football, eight-year-old Paolo constantly refuses to admit faults on his team's side. He argues every time the ball goes out that the other side touched it last. Every time an opposing player touches a member of his team he demands a foul and every time his team behave poorly he refuses to listen. He is very aggressive and domineering in his behaviour and is extremely competitive even with his own teammates, calling them names or being unkind when they make mistakes. He is by no means the best player himself and frequently gives the ball away when he has it because he is unwilling to pass and always wants to be the one to score a goal. Eventually the other children get tired of yet another dispute, the opposing team are constantly giving in on arguments simply to get back to playing and one of the boys on the same team has been reduced to tears.

The children tell Paolo he can no longer play. He tries to intimidate them, but they are adamant. He tries to reason and argue, but they explain that he is no fun to play with and keeps making trouble. They simply carry on without him. He is angry and shouts abuse and calls them names, but they ignore him.

Paolo then went and told an adult, who told the children they had to include him and that they should all play together nicely. At this point the children stopped playing altogether!

Gill comments: a better solution might have been one in which the children were asked to come up with ideas themselves and to identify which of these would be workable. Probably, the only workable solution would have involved a compromise on all parts. Paolo would have to agree to keep quiet and not to argue, and the other children would have to allow him to continue to play. I doubt whether this would work for very long though, and the game would probably break down again. If all the children were available, I would ask each of them to reflect on what happened and why, in a non-blaming way. If only Paolo himself was available, I would ask him to reflect on why the children responded to his choices in the way that they did, and what choices he could make in the future to allow him to participate in the game.

2. Offer more unsupervised play between peers – in safe places such as the garden, in the bedroom or in the park with adults near by (but not with an adult in the middle of them).

Example

Nine-year-old Carly and her sister Amy (aged eleven) share a bedroom at home, so their dad converted the garden shed into a playhouse – no adults allowed – and, as the two girls have different friends, they have a rota for use of the playhouse (alternate days for each sister). The girls may use the playhouse together, but only if the girl whose 'turn' it is allows it. The other girl can, of course, have private use of the bedroom to play under the same rules.

The playhouse is very popular; it has been furnished with old furniture and has a CD player and portable DVD player, as well as plenty of toys. Many of the children who live locally come by regularly and problems have been very few.

Both the girls know they can get help from Mum or Dad should they want it, but are otherwise left alone.

3. Find a better way of dealing with complaints. Don't step in to sort it all out for them; empathise with their difficulties, but don't offer to get involved.

So, if others are not nice to them (or vice versa), allow them the choice not to spend time with them; this gives both parties the chance to change their behaviour rather than adults stepping in to sort it out.

Example

A group of ten-year-old girls are in the school playground. One of them is called Amber. The girls are always falling out with each other and 'taking friends away' from each other. There are no real victims, as sooner or later everyone seems to get sidelined as new loyalties are formed and broken. There are two or three girls who are generally the instigators of splits and seem to enjoy causing rifts in the group. They also seem to enjoy 'making up' and are often in tearful embraces.

One playtime they have split into two camps with one girl, Amber, left out of both. Amber complains to the teacher of being left out and blames everyone else for not sticking up for her. The teacher listens to her complaint and says, 'Poor you. That all sounds really horrible for you. What are you going to do about it?'

Amber is a little put out and says she doesn't know. 'Well what could you do right now, do you think?' asks her teacher. 'What choices do you have?'

Amber suggests that she should be allowed to play with the group and that they should let her.

'Well, I know that's what you want, Amber, but it's not what the others want, is it?'

Amber blusters on a bit about who would like her to play but isn't allowed to because of this or that reason or person.

'I'm sure all that is true, Amber, but I know there have been times when other people have been left out and you have been one of the people leaving them out, haven't you?'

Silence.

'So, we have to think about what you are going to do now. It would be lovely for you to make everybody else behave the way you want, but that is not going to happen. You need to think about the choices you have.'

Eventually, with help, Amber manages to identify a couple of options and decides to go and play with someone else until the problems blow over. She is reunited with her friends the next playtime when another coup takes place and a different girl is left out.

4. Get children to reflect on how they feel when things happen – and then move on to how others may be feeling. The frequent parental starting point of 'How would you feel if . . .' is not helpful to children because many are incapable of putting themselves in someone else's shoes, and almost everyone has problems doing so when under the influence of a strong emotion, such as anger or hurt. You need to teach them how to empathise.

Example
Eleven-year-old Kaleb has just been hit by another boy when he threw the ball they were using to play cricket over a high fence from where it cannot be retrieved. The throw was accidental, but rather careless. The boy who hit him, Alex, is known to have a hot temper. Kaleb runs to his dad who is standing near by.

DAD: How did you feel when you saw the ball go over the fence?

KALEB: Oh it was awful. I knew it was going to go over as soon as it left my hand. I wanted to stop it, but I couldn't.

DAD: How do you think Alex felt when he saw the ball go over the fence?

KALEB: He was really angry. I told him it was an accident, but he hit me.

DAD: Does it make a difference if it was an accident or on purpose?

KALEB: Yes, of course. If I did it on purpose, then I was being horrible, but it was an accident – I couldn't help it.

DAD: Is that what Alex thought?

KALEB: No, he thought I could help it.

DAD: Was he right?

KALEB: Well, I could have done it better, but I didn't mean to lose the ball.

DAD: What do you think Alex could have done differently?

KALEB: He could have just yelled at me.

DAD: Have you ever hit someone for making a mistake?

KALEB: No.

DAD: Are you sure?

KALEB: No, never. Well, maybe.

DAD: I think Alex was wrong to hit you, but can you understand why he did?

KALEB: Yes, but he shouldn't have hit.

DAD: You're right, he shouldn't. What will you do about it?

KALEB: I'm going to tell him he shouldn't have hit.

DAD: What do you think he'll do then?

KALEB: I don't know, but he should say sorry or something.

DAD: What about you? Is there something you might need to say?

KALEB: No, yeah, maybe I should say sorry for losing the ball, even though it was an accident.

Turning negatives into positives

B&C children have many sterling qualities. They are usually fiercely loyal, are not afraid to stick up for something they believe to be right and will champion the underdog against the forces of oppression (you or other adults) as the need arises. While these qualities can be insufferable and annoying, they can also be harnessed for good. B&C adults can, if they wish, change the world – if they can stop getting into rows with all and sundry for long enough!

Similarly, B&C children can learn to use their natural talents for being the centre of attention and speaking fluently and eloquently for the good of all. Encourage your child to get involved in age-appropriate issues by writing to their MP about something they feel strongly about, becoming a member (or chair) of the school council, Local Authority Pupil Parliament or school debating team. Get them to use their skills for good, rather than self-glory. Channel their precociousness, and let them find out how they really can change the world!

Wider social involvement

It's important to get your bright and challenging child to look outside their spotlight into the wider, darker world. And it also needs to start when they are as young as possible, before self-doubt has had a chance to sink in.

TOP TIPS FOR ENCOURAGING WIDER SOCIAL INVOLVEMENT

• Encourage them to have an opinion, on anything and everything. You don't have to agree, and you can, of course, express your views and thoughts or ask some questions to help them develop their opinion. What you must not do is mock or tease them about any expressed opinion, however outlandish. You may ask them to back it up, or reconsider elements if appropriate, but you should commend them and praise them for having thought something through so clearly all by themselves.

• Have discussions with your child about how to make the world a better place – perhaps prompted by a news article or a TV documentary you've watched together.

• Help them to spot the joy in helping others by talking about how good it makes us feel ourselves, such as knowing that you might help to save a life when you give blood. Encourage them to perform spontaneous acts of kindness without any expectation of reward.

• Build on schemes such as those presented on *Blue Peter* or *Children in Need* and encourage them to actively engage others in the same cause.

• Dwell on present giving, and finding the perfect gift, rather than on receiving.

• Help them make things for others – cards, photo albums, cakes, table napkins, mosaic flower pots – anything that would be of particular interest to an individual they know and care for.

• Encourage them to see the whole world as one community, and behaviour in one common pot. Every good thing done, every kindness contributes to the whole in a positive way; every unkindness takes away joy from the common pot.

Questions and answers

Q. *How can I prevent sibling rivalry? My two fight all the time; the youngest, who shows every sign of being a B&C child, is highly competitive and has to win, and this is unfair on his sibling.*
A. Sibling rivalry often stems from a belief that the parent prefers one sibling to another. Interestingly, when sibling rivalry is a real problem, all siblings usually feel that they are the least preferred. If you have brothers and sisters yourself, this is a fascinating topic for discussion!

Their belief is often born out – in their eyes – by the fact that when the pair fight, your attention and sympathy are on the other child. While I can understand how this comes about, every time you show your sympathy for one child over the other, it tends to fan the flames and make the rivalry worse.

Whenever possible, try not to intervene, and let the children sort things out for themselves. Young children need to find a way of dealing with conflict without relying on adults to sort it out for them. It may seem unfair but if your B&C child has got an issue with his brother or sister, let them decide how best to sort it. Eventually, they will find a way of being around each other that works for them.

To young children, love and attention go together; the more attention they get the more loved they feel. Children who feel less loved often display more anger. So make time with each child on their own so they feel loved and valued and you can get to know them even better for being one-to-one.

Q. *My child lies all the time. He has always been verbally able, but as he has got older his stories have got more ingenious and his ability to stick to them, even when they are shown to be* *palpably untrue, has got stronger. The effort of proving what he has said is untrue gets harder all the time.*

A. You have to shift the emphasis away from you having to prove that what he says is untrue to encouraging him to take responsibility for his own actions and tell the truth. This is not about his version of what happened and how far he can keep it going, but about a truth which both parties know and can accept; looking at right and wrong rather than just proof.

Right now he is learning that he can talk his way out of any situation and is getting a power boost from others accepting his lies. Stop asking him for explanations and reasons as they are no longer serving any purpose. If you know he is lying, you do not have to prove it. After all, he knows it too. Simply deal with the behaviour you see and know. He may feel hard done by, but explain to him your reasons – and be absolutely honest about it.

Whenever he tells the truth, however insignificant, praise him. Tell him you can only really be close to him when he is himself and honest and open; the rest of the time, you are being fooled and he is being a liar, so it is not possible for the two of you to really get on with each other. You are both trying to get on with pretend people.

Q. *I heard my child boasting about behaving badly at school and it was clear she was proud of it. Should I confront her about it?*

A. The key point to note is that you overheard it, so you must *not* confront her about it – she has a right to say what she wants to her friends, and what she is saying may not even be true. She may be exaggerating to get a laugh.

Pick your moment, then talk to her about how she feels when others behave badly, such as treating her with no consideration, using inappropriate language, dropping litter and so on. Encourage her to be aware of social boundaries and to see how behaviour that crosses them annoys others. Once she has recognised the point, she can be coaxed to realise how sometimes her own behaviour crosses the line and causes upset or distress to others. Discuss how the 'Other people do it so why shouldn't I?' and 'I wasn't the only one' attitudes affect other people.

Help her to spot the moral high ground and to enjoy moving on to it. B&C children love to be higher than everyone else.

7

GROW UP!

What It Means To Be an Adult and How You Learn It

CHAPTER SNAPSHOT

This chapter will help you to work with your B&C child about what makes a person an adult. It will help you to identify what markers you should be encouraging your child to work towards rather than those popularly celebrated by young people such as partying all night or smoking.

Once we have identified clear markers then the journey towards them also becomes clearer. Knowing which qualities and behaviours show maturity in a person will help you to discuss and explore these issues with your child.

We have also provided a series of milestones for you to consider. These are not intended to be a ruler you measure your child by. Rather they are intended to provide you with a possible framework for encouraging new skills and extending their participation in family life and self-determination.

What does an adult look like to a bright and challenging child?

Bright and challenging children, like all children, vary in behaviour and viewpoint. How they see adults and what they consider to be adult will also vary according to their experience of the adults around them and what they notice along the way. In simpler times, children and adults were clearly identified by the clothes they wore, the way they spent their time, even the food they ate. Around the world such differences can still be seen in some cultures, and special events often mark the movement from one phase of life to another. In our culture, we have no such set markers, although some faith communities still have ceremonies or changes in dress to acknowledge the change in status from child to adult.

Children, however, still want to have a way of showing the world – or each other – that they are growing up, and so will often create markers for themselves. So we have to consider how to encourage children to see themselves becoming adult and rewarding and reinforcing appropriate behaviour and attitudes.

To get some clear views, we did some research with children (many of whom would be considered bright and challenging) about what they thought about adults and becoming an adult. We spoke to groups of children in year two, who were about to enter year three, and other groups in year six, who were just about to go on to secondary school.

In answer to the question, 'What is the difference between a child and an adult?' the younger children said the following:

Adults:
- can boss you about
- can tell children off
- can do what they like
- have more manners
- do the cooking
- watch more TV
- are more boring
- watch the news
- don't do anything interesting
- think more about what to do
- pay taxes

While children, they said:
- have more accidents but get hurt less
- argue more
- cry more
- have better memories
- do more
- sometimes know more
- can't tell adults off
- are more flexible
- are more silly

The children we spoke to were clear in their belief that adults were very 'grown-up and sensible', but that children on the way to being adults were not. The younger children had very well-formed ideas about the distinctions between adults and teenagers.

Adults, they said:
- have a driving licence
- have a job
- are over eighteen/or over twenty-five

- are at college
- start getting pains
- leave home
- have wrinkles
- have a laptop
- have their own house
- have a wife or husband

Whereas teenagers:
- drive against the law
- do illegal things, like breaking and entering and carrying knives
- wear clothes that look cool
- have piercings
- do what they think their parents wouldn't like
- get earrings when they are boys
- have body hair if boys or wax if girls
- use teen language
- swear
- have fake tans
- get drunk
- do anything too early
- wear fake nails
- smoke
- take drugs
- vandalise things
- pretend to talk on the phone
- do graffiti
- take part in dangerous sports to look tough
- argue with the police

So, what does this show us? It would seem that younger children see adults as pretty dull, and that adulthood, while it has its compensations (laptops and driving licences, for example) is really about homemaking and work. While many adults would agree that these do take up a lot of their time, many other aspects of their lives are missing from this picture.

The markers that the younger children identified for teenagers are about being irresponsible and 'wild'. None of the children said they were looking forward to becoming adult but all of them were looking forward to becoming teenagers!

The older children we spoke to had a far more respectful notion of what being an adult meant. For these children, aged about eleven, being an adult had a lot to do with not being childish.

Their answers to the same question – 'What is the difference between a child and an adult?' – showed considerable insight. They replied that:

Adults:
- don't giggle at 'wee' and 'poo' and the word sex
- get bored – their work takes away their imagination and that is the thing that keeps someone childlike (the children mentioned Roald Dahl, who claimed that he had never grown up and had a remarkable and childlike imagination all his life)
- lack spontaneity
- don't play imaginative games with each other

The older children felt that the moment when a child becomes an adult is when they lose their 'childishness' and understanding of children. They also felt that, in some cases, people continue to grow in wisdom as they get older and that this is a lifelong process.

When asked what the first sign of someone growing up was, the children were unanimous in saying that it is when they start going out with someone 'properly' for the first time, as opposed to the 'childish' going out with people that they do when younger. None of them had reached this point yet, though one child had a friend of the same age who had.

The other changes that the older children felt marked someone moving into adulthood were:

- maturing mentally
- growing confidence
- being independent such as by doing own chores, getting a job and ultimately moving out of home
- having their own opinions

The older children felt that adults don't always notice that their children are growing up, even though there are signs that they should be able to pick up on. The most important of these was doing things without being asked, such as emptying the dishwasher or tidying their rooms. However, none of the children we spoke to actually did these things without being asked, but all were adamant that they would when they were older.

Finally, we asked the children in the older group to identify anything they thought young people did to *seem* older. They mentioned:

- wearing make-up
- dressing fashionably
- going to 'older' movies
- going to rock concerts
- showing off
- smoking
- drugs
- violence

- graffiti
- alcohol
- vandalism

To these mainly B&C children growing up to become an adult was all about becoming more sensible and responsible, as well as moving towards more mature and sexual relationships.

It is also useful to reflect upon what the different sexes see as their future attributes in adulthood. What makes a man and what makes a woman.

To children a man:
- is strong
- is sporty
- is brave
- doesn't talk all the time
- reads the paper and watches the news a lot
- eats and drinks more than women
- has an important (to the family) job
- is less committed to the family than women
- is more fun than women

And a woman:
- worries about how she looks all the time/takes care of how she looks
- looks after everyone – cooking, cleaning, washing, childcare, etc.
- is bossy
- talks too much
- flirts
- talks on her phone all the time
- gossips
- likes shopping

That a woman has a job or career was not mentioned. Essentially, the children saw men and women in general very much as they see their own parents. Even those children with successful and career-minded mums didn't seem to see those aspects. (Perhaps they don't talk about their work in front of the children so much?) They felt that men, on the other hand, have more prestigious jobs, yet are still more fun and more irresponsible. This may be because, in the eyes of the children, men have fewer responsibilities in the home where they would experience them. Many children, of course, now grow up without a consistent male role model in the home, and this may be difficult, especially for boys. Spending good-quality time with adults of both sexes is a must for children in helping them to identify the way in which adults behave, and is all part of the socialisation process.

A football coach recently told us that when he is working with groups of boys, he can easily spot those who do have a male role model at home and those who do not. He explained that that those who do will freely chat to him or ask him questions, while those who do not will avoid direct contact.

At what age do we become adults?

In England and Wales the age of criminal responsibility is ten, among the youngest in Europe and the world, while the age of consent is sixteen, one of the oldest. In addition:

- the legal age of 'adulthood' is eighteen
- the age for joining the armed forces is sixteen
- the age for holding a driving licence is seventeen
- a person may vote at eighteen
- you can buy cigarettes and alcohol at eighteen

Even though the legal age of adulthood is eighteen, there is a wealth of evidence that shows young people are not fully mature for some time after this age, in particular in relation to brain development. Processes such as reasoning and choosing actions are not usually fully developed and the thinking process itself is carried out differently in the brains of young people and adults. Some young people are also not fully physically mature until later either, though this varies from individual to individual. Whatever the biological age of maturity may be for the individual, each of us usually has things we remember that marked the moment (or moments) at which we finally felt we had arrived at ourselves – the moments at which we became fully adult.

For many this coincides with the birth of a child:

The first time I held my son in my arms, I knew I was finally grown-up and, like it or not, there was no turning back!

Brian, aged twenty-six

Or it may be associated with with work and career:

When my boss asked my advice on the layout, I felt that I was finally doing it for real, rather than just play-acting at being a grown-up.

Natalie, aged twenty-two

And, for many, feeling like an adult comes even later in life:

It was in my thirties that I finally began to feel grown-up – once the anguish of the teen years had gone, I was in a committed relationship and had children of my own relying on me.

Alison

These may differ enormously from the views we held as children about what it would be like to be adult. So what is an adult? Try the exercise below to see what and how your views of adulthood have changed.

REFLECTION EXERCISE

1. When you were a child what did you look forward to that signified adulthood to you? What did you want that you believed you would or could have as an adult?

_____

_____

_____

_____

_____

_____

_____

2. At which stage in your life did you finally feel fully 'grown-up'? What was it that gave you that feeling or realisation?

_____

_____

_____

_____

_____

_____

_____

Some of the things we have found as markers of adulthood for children include:

- sweets whenever I want them
- not being told what to do
- wearing a bra
- getting up and going to bed when I like
- watching TV all night if I want to
- singing at the end of a school nativity play, with the rest of the audience

Most people will initially find it difficult to remember what they felt constituted being an adult when they were a child. For a lot of people, it will centre around being in control of their own decisions and freedom, or gaining the trappings of assumed maturity, such as certain types of clothing, material possessions or skills and abilities, such as driving a car.

However, for many of us, what finally gave us the feeling of being an adult was something completely different – it was about taking responsibility for ourselves and others, and the realisation that our own (or another's) wellbeing rests on our decisions and our abilities to perform.

Example
Ralph, the father of twelve-year-old Nathaniel and nine-year-old Bianca, identifies his markers of adulthood when he was a child as:

- being able to buy whatever he wanted with his money
- being able to stay out all night
- not having to ask permission before doing anything
- listening to music as loudly as he liked
- eating only the food he liked when he liked and as much as he liked

His moment of realisation came when he brought Nathaniel home from the hospital with his wife. He realised then that he knew nothing about caring for a newborn child, but that he would, and could, do everything in his power to keep the child safe and happy.

Ralph concludes that for children being an adult is about being even more selfish than they are already; while for adults, being an adult is about putting others first. He believes that he can help his children understand adulthood more if he allows them – and expects them – to take more responsibility within the family as they grow older.

Markers of adulthood

Much has been written about the compensation of ageing being the acquisition of wisdom. We discussed with friends, colleagues and anyone else prepared to talk to us what they felt constitutes 'adult' behaviour and thought. Here's what they said.

You are perhaps finally grown-up when:

1. **You can spot patterns in your own behaviour and use them as some sort of learning experience for helping things go better in future.** It can be depressing to look at something that has not worked out – from a conversation to a situation – and suddenly realise that it is part of a pattern, that it has occurred before and that you made the wrong choice last time too. Being a grown-up means recognising that a situation feels familiar as it occurs, and trying to alter the outcome by learning from what went wrong the last time.

There's a Hole in My Sidewalk: Autobiography in Five Short Chapters by Portia Nelson

Chapter I
I walk down the street.
There is a deep hole in the sidewalk.
I fall in.
I am lost . . . I am helpless.
It isn't my fault.
It takes forever to find a way out.

Chapter II
I walk down the same street.
There is a deep hole in the sidewalk.
I pretend I don't see it.
I fall in again.
I can't believe I'm in the same place, but it isn't my fault.
It still takes a long time to get out.

Chapter III
I walk down the same street.
There is a deep hole in the sidewalk.
I see it is there.
I still fall in . . . it's a habit.
My eyes are open.
I know where I am.
It is my fault.
I get out immediately.

Chapter IV
I walk down the same street.
There is a deep hole in the sidewalk.
I walk around it.

Chapter V
I walk down another street.

2. **You can accept that other people don't like you.**
When other people don't like you, it's tempting to
want to change their minds, showing them your
shiny 'best behaviour' to prove just how pleasant
you really are. Being grown-up means having the
self-confidence to just be yourself and accept that
other people may not like it; to understand that
the blockage may be with them, rather than with
you.

3. **You can accept that people's behaviour that
embarrasses you is not your fault, and that you are
not diminished by it.** This means that while you do
have some responsibility for the behaviour of others,
such as children, you are not responsible for the
behaviour of other adults who make their own
choices. You are only responsible for the choice of
being in a relationship with them, not for what they
do.

4. **You understand that you can't live others' lives for
them, and that it's up to them if they want to eat
different things, smoke or make different holiday
choices from you.** We can't all like the same things
or be the same person. The desire to control others
is often a reaction to fear in our own lives – the
fear of life getting out of control. The more
pressures build up and threaten to engulf us the
more we try to control those around us. Parents
experiencing relationship problems, money
problems or work pressures may well try to impose
greater order at home on the things they feel able
to control. When rational, adults understand that
they are not in control, but feelings and

understandings do not come from the same part of our brains. Even when we know that random events can strike at any time we still feel safe when we shut the door!

5. **You can juggle the priorities of many to ensure satisfaction for all.** Children tend to be self-centred and pleasure-seeking, while teenagers are often greedy for experience. They can work out arrangements, but often have little sense of the impact of what they plan on those they live with.

   As an adult, you can encourage co-ordination of plans so that everyone feels their needs have been attended to, and, while you may not mind missing out on the occasional pleasure yourself, you can also insist on what you want to do, without feeling selfish or dominating.

6. **You know when to hold your tongue** . . . and can keep in that comment that points out the fundamental mismatch between words and deeds in the past, in order to preserve the peace. Adults are able to allow others a different viewpoint or opinion without feeling the need to 'correct' it, and without needing the final word. And boy, is this hard sometimes.

7. **You can plan ahead.** Adults can see long-term patterns and predict outcomes, looking further ahead than just the next social event to spot potential dangers that are as yet out of sight. And while this is annoying to children, it's a vital skill to pass on.

I read of some recent research on why it is younger drivers have more road-traffic accidents. It was not the result of poorer driving skills, as one might have expected. Rather, it was a failure to look sufficiently far ahead; to anticipate what might be coming and spot signs, rather than just concentrate on what is close to hand.

It's a good metaphor for teenagers – to encourage them to think about what might be out of sight right now, but will soon be upon them.

Alison

8. **You can manage several things at the same time.** Most of us can concentrate on work or social life, but it's the complicated juggling of several things at the same time that marks out the grown-up. Too much social life and you are useless at work, and too much work and you have no life; balancing the two takes planning and maturity. Arguably, some who are very well supported at work or home never fully achieve grown-up status. Perhaps this is why so many young people who have been brought up with money never seem to grow out of their party lifestyle or manage adult relationships.

9. **You can live with what you have done.** One of the most commonly played pieces of music at funerals is, apparently, 'My Way' (most usually sung by Frank Sinatra). The song recounts failures, problems and successes, but the linking theme is that of making choices. 'Non, je ne regrette rien' by Edith Piaf is a popular funeral song in the French-speaking world too, for similar reasons.

Being an adult means changing what can be

changed and living with what cannot, and, in the words of the Serenity Prayer (commonly attributed to the theologian Reinhold Niebuhr), 'the wisdom to know the difference'.

Helping children to pass milestones

Parents have to allow children to develop responsibility for themselves by doing things themselves. It is undoubtedly true that in most cases it is easier, quicker and creates less mess to do things for them. However, they will not learn self-reliance by watching you, they will learn it by having to think things through for themselves. Recently, Gill was in the foyer of a secondary school at about eleven in the morning, waiting to meet with a member of staff. While she was there, no fewer than three mothers arrived to bring in items their child had forgotten to take with them to school that morning. There was also one young person who came in asking for permission to phone home for something to be brought in.

While we have sympathy for those parents who don't want their child to have the embarrassment or disapproval of teachers, by taking away all consequence from the act of forgetting they are not helping their child to take responsibility for their own belongings and needs at school one bit.

We learn by reflecting on the consequences of our actions, by seeing 'what happens if' and deciding on the best outcome for our effort. B&C children have trouble learning by consequence anyway, as they tend to blame everyone and anyone before accepting that they may have been at fault, but by bailing them out each time, you are simply reinforcing their view that it is not their responsibility to sort things out but someone else's 'job'. As one child put it: 'She had me; I didn't choose to be born. So it's her job to take care of me.'

Children tend to view being an adult as being a child with the boundaries taken away, so getting them to dwell on, and giving them practical experience of, how it is in reality is important, i.e. that being an adult requires you to take responsibility for yourself. They need to understand that, in fact, society is full of rules and that adults are grown-up because they understand their importance.

For many of us as children, becoming an adult was not discussed much. Adulthood was tied in closely with the securing of work and money; our parents controlled the purse strings and that gave them the last word in all things. Until we contributed, we had no right to choose anything or make long-term decisions. Today's children still see money as a big difference between adults and children, but have less understanding of how it is earned or what having (or not having) it means beyond the short term.

Setting milestones for your children

The milestones below are simply suggestions as to what we feel is appropriate and provide a suitable challenge to a child when growing up. You might like to use them as a basis for discussion with your partner and children.

By the age of eleven, a child should be able to:

- get his or her own equipment ready for school, e.g. PE kit, books
- do homework without being nagged about it
- remember to take their own lunch – or ask for money for it – rather than being reminded; perhaps make it too
- put laundry in the basket
- wash up their own breakfast things/put them in the dishwasher

- manage their personal hygiene – not need to be reminded about when to shower etc.
- start to plan their own social lives and suggest arrangements; negotiate over family commitments, rather than informing at the last minute that they are going out
- practise for things they have said they want to do and show commitment to attending (things they have been signed up to by their parents, e.g. piano lessons, may need more negotiation)
- accept that there are times when they have to be part of the family, even when the plan is not to their liking
- allow siblings to say and do things they don't like without reacting

By the age of fourteen, they should be able to:

- manage everyday friendships and relationships
- support friends who are in difficulties, but understand the boundaries between supporting them and telling them what to do
- talk through problems, about work, social life, and with the most appropriate people and at the right time
- manage themselves – know how to do their own laundry, know how to iron, to cook the odd meal (or at least know the principles of healthy eating)
- contribute at home – do tidying, cleaning, vacuuming, mowing lawn, corner shopping when things are forgotten, walk the dog
- contribute to the overall smooth running of the household
- put away shopping or go shopping with whoever does it and help to pack it up

- get to school on time and under their own steam
- be aware of their grades and what they have to do to pass/move up a level
- understand their potential, and maybe have developed some plans for the future
- make healthy choices – food, spending, drinking and smoking; also, independent thinking – so not just doing what everyone else does
- understand timing – eating, exercising, coming back at sensible times
- plan, take and pass on messages, write things on the family calendar so they don't get forgotten
- plan ahead for weekends and summer holidays – checking with parents first that there are no clashes
- develop a sense of family loyalty and support/stick up for family members; talk about their positive attributes, rather than just moan about those they live with
- behave responsibly by keeping to curfews, giving honest details of schedules and whereabouts
- stay in contact when out
- be truthful with parents even in difficult circumstances

By the age of sixteen, they should be able to:

- respect their parents' care for them, i.e. come up with their own plans, but let their parents know what is in place, and when they will be back, etc; also respect their desire to keep them safe
- understand the importance of honesty, so that in the case of emergency they can be found when they are out (e.g. by leaving their phone switched on)
- manage their own laundry and ironing (boys and girls)

- help at home; clean up after themselves and also help to clean up after others, not just add to the general mess or clutter
- choose friends according to whether the relationship is in their interests or not
- be discerning in relationships and able to manage new ones too, rather than sticking to the same set of friends
- be open-minded
- demonstrate good social skills with new people
- show some discernment in attraction-based relationships, e.g. not accept all invitations, but choose in a considered way
- reflect on why they find someone attractive (and why not), i.e. not allowing themselves to be wholly emotion- and hormone-led (see Chapter 9)
- talk problems in relationships through with people – including parents – with politeness
- communicate with parents without shouting
- recognise when they have made a mistake, and apologise for it; also, forgive others who have made a mistake
- take full responsibility for homework, study time and exams at school or college and ask for help or support if needed – from parents or teachers
- plan for the future and research into it; think maturely about what they want to do, rather than waiting to be told

By the age of twenty, they should be able to:

- be independent for long periods of time and manage on their own
- be trusted, e.g. if you go away on holiday and leave

them at home, you should be able to trust them to manage the home and respect your property and values

- eat properly, manage laundry, look after personal hygiene, keep living space tidy, keep up with work and study, as well as social life – managing the two and keeping lots of things on the go at the same time is not easy
- make and break attraction-based relationships; recognise that a relationship is not working and be able to move on in a kindly way, rather than staying in it because they are afraid they won't find another one
- show consideration for others – accept that others have different points of view and hear them without feeling that they have to prevail
- be kind and do things to please others, e.g. remember birthdays, turn up for special events, phone to cheer other people up – not just because they want something, care for friends
- understand reasons and responsibilities, and that they can't always do just what they want; understand that others may rely on them
- manage without, e.g. if they have spent all their allowance, accept that they can't have all they want; hold money back for specific instances (e.g. late-night taxi) and manage to stick to what they had planned
- show self-discipline
- (if in work) get there on time without needing to be reminded; or (if studying) get their assignments in on time or spot deadline clashes and negotiate around them ahead; schedule based on experience of own character and time available; understand their

preferred method of work and study (last minute/forward planning)
- reflect and achieve self-knowledge
- take criticism and act on it, rather than just hating the person who gave it; think about what it means and how changes can be made
- care about the community and those they have never met; demonstrate altruism; societal and civic awareness (e.g. vote, read information on candidates whether in national or student/local elections; take part)
- keep safe; understand risk and make choices that support wellbeing on a day-to-day basis

These milestones (or your own modified version) can be used in conjunction with your child's demands for greater freedoms and privileges. These should be given when a youngster has shown themselves to be mature enough to handle them and not just when they reach a certain age.

Questions and answers

Q. *My ten-year-old son is forever leaving things he needs for school at home – which means that I am forever running into school with what he has forgotten.*
A. If you are providing such a comprehensive back-up service, what incentive does he have to remember in future? Don't cover the gaps in his memory; rather let him find out the consequences of forgetting first hand – it will probably make him less likely to forget in future.

Q. *It's mayhem in our house in the morning – my eleven-year-old son won't get up, won't eat breakfast, and is in constant*

danger of missing his school bus. By the time he leaves the
house, I feel quite worn out.
A. Buy him an alarm clock and a personal organiser chart to
go on the wall of his bedroom. Give him one call only and
leave it at that. Make absolutely clear that he knows this is
all you are going to do in the future. He has to understand
that it's up to him – not you – to create a realistic schedule
for getting himself to school on time, and while you should
support him in developing organisational skills, that does
not mean taking over the organisation for him. The transition to secondary school is the ideal time to start a new
regime of independence.

Q. *My daughter says she can't wait until she is fourteen so that
she can do what she likes – because by then she will be bigger
than me. This is worrying me; because I am not tall, I am sure
she will soon be bigger than me, and I will feel even more physically intimidated than I do now. What should I do?*
A. You don't say how old your daughter is now and that is
quite significant. But you do mention that you are already
somewhat physically intimidated.

Your daughter seems to think that physical power and
aggression are what makes one person in control and
another subservient. Where can this idea have come from?
How has she decided that this is how the world works?

Whatever the answer to that question, it is time now to
change things, and hopefully she is not so old that she
cannot relearn. She needs to understand your role as her
carer and parent and why you do what you do. She also
needs to understand respect within relationships and what
that means and looks like. Always use please and thank you
to her, refrain from overly criticising, rather ask for specific
changes in her behaviour.

So don't, for example, say: 'You are such a messy eater.

Look at the state of that table. I don't know why you have to be so careless and thoughtless. And I bet you're not going to clean it up either are you? Oh no. That'll be my job!' Rather, try: 'Please eat your food over the plate, so any bits fall on to it, rather than on the table.' And when she makes an effort to remember to do this, praise her.

Help her also to see that the world has certain risks and dangers in it, and that she needs to take time to learn and grow before she is able to take them on. Discuss things with her often and listen to her viewpoints, even if you disagree with them. Put across your own thoughts calmly.

Be firm but fair with your boundaries, and don't let her intimidate or browbeat you into changing them once they are set. Be prepared to negotiate them though, as she grows older.

8

STREET SMART

Preparing Your Child to Recognise and Manage Risk

CHAPTER SNAPSHOT

In this chapter we will look at how you, as parents, talk to your children while they are young about risk, so that they are equipped when older to assess risk in a more realistic and less impulsive way.

As we have already seen, the B&C child is particularly at risk in some areas because of their natural precociousness and tendency to want to try new experiences younger. And, because they are more independent, and often look and act older than their years, it's not unusual for them to be treated as older. Add to this their desire to stand out from the crowd at all costs, and you can see that they are potentially even more at risk; particularly if they find themselves in the company of other risk-takers.

What are risks?

By risk we mean any activity or action which has the potential to result in harm, and this includes physical, emotional or social harm such as physical damage, embarrassment or shame and being excluded from friendships.

Physical risks

When adults think about risks in the context of young people, they think almost entirely of the physical risks that they may face: drugs, knives, alcohol, accidents, violence, sexual assault and unprovoked attack. All of these are threats to the physical wellbeing of their child, and of course they want to protect them from harm as much as they can.

Adults face distressing images in the media of the consequences of risk-taking among the young on a daily basis. They have images in their minds of crumpled car wrecks and small coffins carried by grieving families. They know what damage a speeding car can do to a child on a bicycle or how the funeral of yet another knifed teenager would look.

But with their much more limited life experience, and no concept of mortality in relation to themselves, children have little thought for danger, and cannot picture it in their minds. B&C children, in particular, have a strong sense of self-reliance that makes them think they can handle pretty much anything that comes their way.

Take, for instance, the image of children playing 'chicken' on railway lines or climbing too high. As a parent, you can imagine the next frame in the sequence where the child is hit or falls; you can hear the noise and see the what-happens-next pictures in your mind. This is what stops you taking too many risks for yourself and trying to restrict your child's actions too.

Asked what might happen as a consequence of playing on the railway line or climbing too high, the child can probably describe a similar sequence if coaxed to do so, but is much more likely to be caught up in the moment; enjoying the thrill – provided as much by the fact that the action is forbidden as it is by the possible consequences. They lack the ability and experience to visualise this frightening image, or to see their action in the context of a series of events that could move out of their control. Most children think their parents are over-sensitive about the risks they face.

Social and emotional risks

When children are younger, their understanding of risk is purely physical: what can hurt you. Much of this may come from parents but much is learnt by cause and effect. So children have to learn what hurts them – that falling down hurts, that falling down from higher up hurts more, that too hot and too cold can hurt, that sharp things can cut, and so on. While there is a strong tendency for modern parents to 'cotton-wool wrap' their children to curtail this process, children's nature will out and most of them will manage to cut, scrape, bump, burn, freeze and twist themselves – and so learn about everyday risks.

But as children grow older, their priorities change. By the time they reach eleven or twelve, i.e. shortly before adolescence, they begin to worry far less about physical risk and more about the social and emotional risks of everyday life.

Social risks are anything that affects their standing with their peer group. When children start secondary school at eleven, as most do, their friendship groups are fairly fluid. While they may have had some very close friendships, they tend not to be scared about losing casual friends, as they feel confident about making new ones among the many children around them.

As they get older, and friendship groups become more fixed, a young person who leaves or is pushed out of their friendship group may not find it easy to get into another, already-established grouping. This causes some anxiety for many young people and is one of the main reasons why they stay with friends who are 'mean' to them or who treat them unfairly, rather than moving on to make new friends. The fear of social isolation or rejection is very real for young people, particularly girls, who have a good understanding of social networking and what it means to be outside the system through the endless make-or-break friendship battles they go through in their middle to late primary-school years. (Years three to four are notorious in most schools for the girlie friendship wars.)

Because of their desire to be seen at all costs, B&C children understand what it means to be top dog or outsider as they have probably experienced both. While they would rather be the wild loner than an also-ran, their chosen position would usually be one of 'Lord of all I survey'. When this is not possible they may well decide to go it alone as cynical wise-cracker, uber-trendy or even super-geek.

What really terrifies the B&C child is being ridiculed and embarrassed. This emotional risk is a potent fear for all young people but especially for the B&C child who will probably never truly learn to laugh at themselves the way most people do. Gill has met young people who have sworn never to go back to school because they tripped and fell on the steps and were laughed at, or because they gave a foolish answer to a question and were humiliated by the teacher's response, which caused the class to laugh.

Humiliation is undoubtedly one of the strongest and most uncomfortable emotions a person can experience; it is right up there with grief and shame as emotions we avoid whenever possible. It also has the power to return throughout our lives and still cause discomfort thirty, forty or even fifty years down the line.

Try the exercise below – you'll need to be brave for this one, but you also stand to learn a lot!

REFLECTION EXERCISE

Can you remember one time when a teacher humiliated you?

What were you doing?
What did they say?
How did you feel?

Can you remember one time when you were with friends and you suffered a humiliation?

Where were you?
Who did what?
How did you feel?

Can you remember one time when a parent or other close family member humiliated you?

What did they do?
How did you feel?
How did this affect your relationship with them?

Feedback
Adults reflecting on this have said:

One of my abiding memories is of when I was in secondary school. My Italian teacher asked me a question, and I didn't know the answer. The teacher made me stand on a chair in front of the whole class. I was twelve. He asked questions all around the room, and every time someone got a question wrong he hit *me* across the hand with a ruler.

What made it even worse was that my mum didn't believe me when I told her what had happened. I started getting panic attacks at night. I hated Italian. When that teacher left I never did a single bit of homework or coursework again. I failed Italian.

Gill

I was about ten. We were playing in the park with the ball. Some big boys came along and started kicking the ball about, so we couldn't play any more. I got really angry and started shouting at them. They started to tease me and call me names, and I got more and more angry. In the end, even my friends started to laugh at me because I was being so cross and stomping about. I got so frustrated I started crying, and that was the end of it! I never lived it down. I think it was years before I went to that park again and most of the boys I'd been playing with were no longer my friends from that day on.

Raymond

I was about seven or eight and I was at a family party – I don't remember why. My mum called me over and said my tights were crooked. She then lifted up my skirt, took down my tights and made me sit down while she put them on again like I was a three-year-old. All the time, she was talking to the other adults. I was horrified and really ashamed. I used to make a real fuss about going to family parties after that and I always wore trousers until I was in my twenties.

Fiona

The power of humiliation

Remembering humiliation can be almost as painful as the original event. Of all the memories that we have, humiliation stays among the most potent and powerful. As a result of humiliation, many of us will have changed the way we behave for ever, putting rules into operation to prevent ourselves from ever feeling that way again. We may harbour a deep and abiding hatred for the person or people we blame for that humiliation.

Sometimes, humiliation is used as a way of bringing home a harsh lesson to a child or curbing their behaviour, and it's certainly true that they will probably never forget the moment, associating it with feelings of distress and lasting resentment, as well as some trauma. But the lesson they have learnt may not be the one intended. Gill didn't get better at Italian, Raymond didn't learn to laugh at himself with his friends and Fiona didn't learn to put her tights on straight. (Although there is no suggestion in her story that Fiona's mother was intentionally trying to humiliate her.)

Most people would be very unwilling today to use humiliation deliberately as a way of controlling a child's behaviour. And the risks of using it with the B&C child are particularly high. Most such children are acutely sensitive to hurt (although not necessarily to the feelings of others). To retain an intimate and caring relationship with a B&C child it is important to avoid behaviour or criticism which they might experience as humiliating.

Away from home, it is this fear of humiliation that might keep a young person from saying 'No thanks' when offered a share of some cocaine at a party, or pausing play when a snogging session goes further than they had intended. Many young people would rather take the risk – be it an unknown substance, pregnancy or a lift from a stranger – than risk ridicule. And the stock argument of those urging less caution – 'What's the matter, are you afraid?' – still works on today's young person, as it has for generations. It can get someone to commit an act they might otherwise have stayed away from, just to avoid being laughed at or teased.

Gill recalls an incident where a twelve-year-old boy had stuck a compass point right through the webbing between his thumb and forefinger as a dare. He needed hospital treatment and course of tetanus injections as a result. This is an extreme but fairly typical example of the lengths someone will go to to gain a certain reputation with friends and peers and to avoid ridicule as a coward.

Feelings of embarrassment and humiliation are extremely hard to deal with, regardless of age. For some out-of-control young people, they are triggers to lashing out verbally or physically at whoever has 'disrespected' them, which, in most cases, means criticised or laughed at them. For B&C children, such feelings are almost impossible to manage. They are never willing to look at themselves and find fault, and find it unbearable when someone else does. They may retaliate excessively and may hold grudges for a long time.

Example

When she was seven, Bethany failed to blow out all the candles on her birthday cake in one go after boasting confidently that she could. Several of her friends commented or laughed at the time, and her older sister Louise made a big deal out of it, mocking her for boasting, and teasing her about it for days afterwards.

After the incident, Bethany behaved badly, got into lots of rows with people and upset many of her friends, most of whom went home as early as they could. Bethany was very upset with her sister and blamed *her*; both for the failure in blowing out the candles and everything that went wrong subsequently.

Now, two years on, at Louise's thirteenth birthday party – a milestone party with a lot of preparation, Bethany is seen by her mum squirting washing-up liquid into the punch bowl. She is clearly taking revenge.

It is possible that Bethany doesn't even remember the details of the incident at her own birthday party. She probably hasn't been planning to get her own back all this time. But what has taken place is that Bethany harbours a deep dislike of her sister and wants to ruin her big day.

One of the ways in which some people deal with social and emotional risk, probably from childhood onwards, is to suppress any emotion and isolate themselves socially. This way they cannot get hurt and will never have to suffer humiliation or disappointment again. Seeing a child do this, even for a short period, can be very distressing, but a few days will cause no harm. However, the problem can be more worrying with B&C children, who are often not socially resilient beings and can take a very long time to lick their wounds.

If the behaviour lasts longer than a few days you might be able to help by getting them to open up a bit about the original hurt. Asking them to talk about it probably won't work, but asking an opinion on so-and-so's behaviour might. Bethany's mum (see example above) could have got her to talk about what she thought of Louise and helped her to offload some of her anger and shame. Sharing a similar experience to theirs from your own early life might help your child to feel less of an outcast, particularly if you can find one that shows both how you felt vulnerable and how you dealt with your feelings in the longer term.

One of the aspects of a B&C child's behaviour that most distances them from their peers is that when a course of action fails to get the required response, rather than backing down and shutting up they tend to just keep going. This can lead to embarrassment heaped upon embarrassment for them and make back-tracking difficult. They may end up feeling very unhappy and confused, having taken a course of action way further than they could handle – or even really wanted to. Most of us see the impact of our behaviour and make adjustments accordingly, but a B&C child may be so stubborn that they find this difficult to do, and are likely to keep going regardless.

CASE STUDY

Eleven-year-old Nasir told his school friends on the way to school that his sister had been in a car accident at the weekend. This was not true. He was simply trying to get attention from the group, so went all out to top all the other kids' stories.

One of the children then told his form tutor who called Nasir aside to ask how his sister was and to offer support. Nasir claimed she was seriously injured and in hospital. Having enjoyed the attention, the next day he told his classmates that she was dead. He asked them to keep the information to themselves, claiming he did not want anyone else to know. When the form tutor was informed, he immediately contacted the family to offer condolences and support. It was at this point that he was told that there had been no accident.

Nasir's parents were understandably horrified that their son had made up such a terrible story. His sister was doubly upset to think that he had disposed of her to suit his own ends so callously.

The school spent quite a lot of time and energy with Nasir to help him identify what had led him to this course of behaviour, and at what point it became unmanageable. He was helped to find other ways of getting attention both in a crowd and from adults, and for getting out of difficult situations if he should ever find himself feeling the need to add bigger and bigger lies to extricate himself.

The multiplier: understanding risk in the context of time

Not only do you need to help B&C children understand the notion of the various kinds of risks they face, you also need to help them appreciate how the assessment of risk is affected by time. Some things may seem, or be, of little risk at one moment but of high risk at another time. Crossing a road, for instance, varies from moment to moment according to traffic conditions; accepting a lift from a friend may be one thing at lunchtime, but quite another after a party at which alcohol has been consumed.

Some risks exist only in the future, such as the risk of smoking cigarettes. When a person starts smoking, there is almost no immediate risk to them, but, as time goes by, the risks increase. Twenty years further down the road, the ingrained habit and long-term associated health problems have made smoking a seriously risky behaviour.

Likewise, though even harder for young people to grasp, is the risk of eating badly or having too much 'junk food'. Right now, the risks may seem minor, but again, as time goes by, the problems posed by poor nutrition and obesity, with the associated reduction in activity and exercise, become potentially life-threatening. It's not just young people who find the time-delay risks tricky – everyone does to some degree. We all fall for the bit of chocolate cake when we aren't hungry or the takeaway when we are too tired to prepare food. We have nearly all had a drink too many or driven somewhere when we could have walked, and so on. The problem with time-delay risks is that while each individual incident is of little consequence, and for the most part 'just one won't hurt', it's the repetition over years and years that makes them harmful.

Children and young people have little sense of the future and so they are unlikely to put something that may cause them one kind of risk in twenty years' time above something that may cause them a different kind of risk today. The risk of being teased by their peers for not having a drag on a cigarette at ten will feel far greater to them in that moment than the prospect of lung disease at fifty. At nine, the risk of alienation and criticism carried by saying no to spending the money they have been given for breakfast at school on a breakfast menu at McDonald's may be a greater concern than that of heart disease when they are forty.

Help your child to manage risks

The most important way in which all children learn to manage risk is by taking risks in small steps, a bit at a time, and learning to manage situations as they arise.

So the six-year-old may go to the end of the road alone to post a letter, the eight-year-old may go to the local shop alone across the zebra crossing and the eleven-year-old may go to school alone when they start secondary school. It is a normal part of a child's development that they become more independent as they get older and want to have experiences away from parents and family.

Unfortunately for the parent of a B&C child, not all children develop at the same rate and a B&C child may want far more independence than their parents are willing to give them and feel extremely confident that they can manage all life might throw at them. Having said that, we have met bright and challenging children who were excessively nervous of the world from an early age, and their precocity had led to them learning far more than was healthy for them about potential dangers. Gill remembers one eight-year-old girl who was at risk of becoming agoraphobic because she was so aware of every danger that might befall her, as a result of her anxious mother repeatedly telling her horror stories of abductions, assaults, murders and rapes.

Today's children are more apprehensive of 'strangers' than any other generation has been, and seeing a kindly older person making a friendly comment to a child only to be met with hostile stares is very sad. Getting the balance right is important and can be challenging. Helping children to distinguish between safe, possibly risky and risky takes time and relies on good communication and repetition.

It also relies on parents taking time to think themselves about what the levels of risk really are. Thankfully, the things parents dread most are extremely rare, even if the media make them seem as if there is a monster or catastrophe waiting around every corner. It is still true that more children are hurt in their own homes than outside, most sexual abuse is by a member of the family or friend of the family and children are more at risk in their parents' car than they are walking. Wrapping them in cotton wool will not help them to keep safe. The day will come when they will be out on their own, and, if they have not learnt any 'streetwise' tactics they will be more at risk than their peers.

One of the things you have to do is to help children work out ways of reducing risks rather than avoiding them all together. Even the terrible events that are often reported in the press could sometimes have been prevented or made less risky had certain actions been taken (hindsight is so easy). Encourage children to verbalise these, but avoid extremes. So, 'If he hadn't gone out in the first place', is not helpful, but, 'If he had stayed with his friends and not gone off alone', may be more instructive.

Whenever your children go anywhere there will be some risk – none of us is able to control the world around us. So it's a good idea to ask them to think about what could go wrong and how that could be managed. For example, if they are going swimming with a friend in the local pool, ask them what would they do if they got to the pool and it was unexpectedly closed? What would they do if someone picked on them in the pool? What would they do if they lost their locker key? How they would get home if they were unable to phone home for a lift when they were ready, as planned?

This may sound like an interrogation written on the page, but it can be a fun exchange with more ridiculous and extreme problems being added to the list. ('What would you do if the Olympic team was there training and only one of you got asked to join their session?') Once you are happy that they know how to manage the unexpected, *you* will feel better about them going too.

Managing 'time-delay' risks

In some respects, B&C children are easier to work with on this one as they are smart and grasp ideas quickly, as well as being – generally – very willing to pass on their wisdom about risk management to their peers, should the opportunity arise. Gill has witnessed several occasions where a B&C child has held forth on issues relating to health, regardless of, or even spurred on by, the eyebrow-raising and scowling of their peers.

It's necessary to introduce such children to the longer-term risks associated with certain behaviours, as is discussing with them the impact of unpopular choices in the present. As they get older, they will find many situations where they will have to make choices that might cause them embarrassment but which may save them from harm in some form in the future. So they need to be prepared in advance for what to say and do if situations arise. Encourage them to think through for themselves their position on a range of issues, then probe a little further by asking, 'What would you do if . . .' or, 'What would you say then if . . .'

Take, for example, the issue of a child lying to a parent as to their whereabouts. Ask your nine-year-old what they think about someone who goes out in the evening and tells their parents that they are at a friend's house when in reality they are at an all-night party. Then try to get them to articulate:

- why they think this person may have lied
- what the rewards are for the lie and what the risks are
- what else could this young person have done
- what they would do if in similar circumstances they wanted to do something but thought that their parent would not agree
- what they would do if a friend said they were a coward or a baby for not going along with such a plan

As they work their way through the problems from all sides, praise their thoughtfulness and reasoning. Ask questions to encourage them to see the issue from all angles, not just your own. For example, how will siblings interpret what has happened, and how about the parents of the young person who is providing an alibi for the party?

Again, this may look on the page a bit like an interrogation, but most B&C children enjoy working their way through moral and social dilemmas, especially if they think you have not got all the answers. Make a game of it – 'Here's a tricky problem for you' – and play in the car on the way to the supermarket or when walking to school in the morning. As time goes by, add in some issues that concern drugs and sex. Use the newspapers as a good starting point, or the endless reservoir of issues that is the soap opera.

Managing physical risk

Physical risk, like beauty, is in the eye of the beholder. Parents sometimes see risk lurking round every corner while children may be blissfully unaware in almost any circumstance.

A physical risk is any risk to the bodily wellbeing of the child. Traffic must constitute one of the largest risk factors in our everyday world and accidents of all kinds generally still cause most harm to children's physical wellbeing. It is important to remember that if children are to learn to manage physical risk they need to have real experience. Being told what to do, being warned of what might happen and being scared by examples do not teach a child coping skills.

When a child is young managing their physical risk is a parent's responsibility which is taken up in turn by schools. Having good boundaries, obeying commands (such as stop!) and staying close to an adult are all ways of keeping a child safe. As children get older and start to explore the world more on their own, keeping them safe becomes harder. Of all children, the B&C child will be most eager to try new things, although not all B&C children are physically brave. Many prefer the world of words.

Helping children manage physical risk is about keeping their boundaries tight while teaching them to notice potential dangers and to make choices accordingly. As they show increased awareness and maturity, so we allow the boundaries to slacken. If they mess up or forget the rules then we tighten the boundaries again. For example, a child of eight who wishes to make some cheese on toast will be allowed to do so if an adult is standing by. That adult will point out the dangers of touching hot surfaces, the importance of turning the gas off after completion and how to use a knife correctly when cutting something as hard as cheese.

By the age of eleven the child may be allowed to make their cheese on toast by themselves after a quick rundown on the safety procedures. If, however, they leave the gas on then the next time they ask it will be back to being supervised throughout.

Managing social risk

Social risks are those terrible gaffes we all make at some time or another that lead us to feel embarrassed or humiliated (and so link with emotional risks). A social risk is any action that has the potential to lead to being singled out in a negative way by our peer group or others we care about.

The B&C child is particularly vulnerable to social risk as their impulse is always to be seen as different. Too different and they become unacceptable, too much the same and they feel unremarkable.

Help your child to notice the effect that their behaviour and choices have on others around them; when things have gone well, encourage them to think about why (they will find this easier than when things have gone badly). What did they do that led to everyone having such fun or enjoyment? Help them to recognise in themselves behaviour that others respond to well or badly. Begin to help them to recognise the range of choices that people make in relation to their behaviour with or around others and how this links to their 'popularity'.

Avoid giving direct negative feedback or criticism, such as,

'It was really mean of you to tell Josie that her dress was ugly.' If you give your B&C child negative feedback the most common response will be for them to hate you or feel that they have been treated unfairly, rather than to reflect on their own behaviour. Encourage their opinions and observations about how social situations have worked/could have worked better. Give lots of praise for their insights.

Managing social risk is essentially about balancing the desire to fit in and the desire to stand out. Helping your B&C child to understand this will be invaluable to them. Even a simple technique like drawing up a 'for' and 'against' list may help them make decisions.

Example

Ten-year-old Phoebe has a friend, Natalie, over for tea. She is very controlling and insists on telling Natalie what she can and cannot do at each moment. Phoebe chooses exactly what the girls do and how Natalie is to behave. While showing her 'jewellery' collection she doesn't allow her to touch anything and tries all sorts of hairstyles with her collection of clips and slides, but won't allow Natalie to try any or to use her brush. Natalie is a quiet and passive girl but is clearly feeling quite bored; she leaves earlier than originally planned.

What *not* to do: 'Well that's the last time I'm letting you invite a friend for tea. I'm so embarrassed that she called her mum to ask her to come and collect her early. She was obviously not having any fun and you were horrible to her. I shall never be able to look Natalie's mum in the eye again in the playground. Why do you have to be so horrible?'

The clever approach: 'What things did you do with Natalie? What do you think she might have liked to do more? What can we do to have fun with Natalie and her mum, so they will still want to be our friends?'

Looking to the future, plan a fun day out together – a visit to a local park or exhibition that will involve both child and mother; this will provide a useful mechanism for exploring social skills, and stimulus can be provided by the venue and not just the child. A debriefing on the way home about how it went might help to consolidate what worked and what didn't in a shared and, therefore, non-blaming way.

Managing emotional risk

Emotional risks are those events or incidents that might result in a child feeling hurt, angry, disappointed or over-whelmed by an uncomfortable or unpleasant emotion. They are things that leave the child with a lasting emotional pain.

One way to manage emotional risk is to develop a greater emotional resilience – an ability to withstand knockbacks, criticism or any other aspect of the behaviour of others. The greater the resilience, the easier social interaction becomes until it reaches a point, sometimes seen in B&C children, where it no longer matters at all what anyone else thinks or does. At such a time I think we can say that resilience has become arrogance and greater empathy is needed.

Interestingly B&C children are at either end of the resilience spectrum. Many are desperately hurt by even the most careful criticism (while dishing out judgements on others all over the place). Others barge through any resistance or attempt at negotiation with contempt and assurance in their own stance no matter what. For both these extremes we need the child to understand not only their own emotions but also those of others. We need them also to understand and respect the universality of emotions.

Encourage the recognition of feelings by being honest about how you feel and specific about your own emotions – this helps your child to recognise them, rather than just feeling that you are, say, angry all the time. This is harder than it sounds: to do it you need to learn to 'unpick' your own emotional response. For example, you may feel angry, but on reflection find that this anger is really a mixture of frustration, stress, tiredness, hurt and disappointment. Get used to naming all your feelings when they are relevant, not just the ones that are stimulated by your child's behaviour.

Secondly, encourage them to identify emotions in themselves and to be specific about how *they* are feeling. We often feel a mixture of feelings all jumbled up together and at times these can be, or seem to be, conflicting. It's OK to have a muddle of feelings all going on at once – even though it may be uncomfortable. Help your child to identify their feelings rather than sorting them out for them; try to get them to see how, perhaps, making different choices could have altered the outcome and the way they are feeling right now. It is not our job to make them happy when they are not; rather to help them understand the causes for their unhappiness and how they can make choices to avoid the emotional consequence next time around or make choices in the present to change how they feel.

The simplest and most obvious strategy in helping a child to develop their emotional literacy is to teach them the words you use to describe your feelings. Many children struggle to put into words how they feel because they simply don't know the words in the first place. At about age five, children can rarely name more than happy, sad, angry and frightened, but by age eight they should be able to use many more. How many words can you identify?

HOW MANY EMOTIONS CAN YOU LIST IN FOUR MINUTES?

_____

_____

_____

_____

_____

_____

_____

Feedback

How well did you do? Most parents who've done this task have come up with a maximum of around 24–26. Meanwhile, the Science Museum website claims there are over six hundred words in English to describe emotions.

Try this with your child too – see how many they can come up with. Perhaps you can learn some new ones together? Here are some other ways in which you can help them to develop their emotional repertoires:

- Get them to notice different emotions in others. Use films, television, incidents with the neighbours or in the local paper as a starting point if their own experience is too difficult for them. B&C children may clam up or become spiteful or defensive if they feel criticised

- Encourage them to think about how others feel. 'Why did so and so react that way?' Get them to explore 'how it would feel if . . .' and encourage them to empathise with a situation they can observe either on TV or in real life. Asking them, 'How do you think I felt when . . .' is a question parents often ask, but it will almost never work. The B&C child can empathise with others but only when they are not directly involved. Any emotion they have themselves experienced in a situation will override their ability to empathise with someone else

- Talk to them about how they can and do show emotion in different ways – and not just to get attention and sympathy from others. They will learn more from this than by either being told how they feel (as in: 'You're very angry right now, so just . . .') or having their feelings suppressed by adults (as in: 'Now just calm down and relax')

- Encourage them to reflect on how they feel about news stories. Listen to their views and give your own, as well as encouraging other family members to join in. Show that you value each person's views by not making judgements about whether what they say is right or wrong, but by giving praise for their reasoned opinions, thoughtfulness and ability to understand others

Questions and answers

Q. *There have been several incidents in the area where I live, and as a result I don't want my children going out to play unsupervised. Yet you are saying they should be allowed to take risks and be on their own sometimes. I can't do both.*
A. If you are feeling like this, presumably there are others who do too. So can you work around this together – maybe by making a play rota to go to the park, play area or green space with adults taking turns to provide supervision? Can you let the children play there together with some degree of

autonomy, so that even if arguments break out between them the adults will try to let them resolve things themselves without sorting it out for them?

Encourage them to join groups that do collective activities – Brownies and Cubs, Guides and Scouts, Girls' Brigade, Woodcraft Folk, youth clubs and pre-youth clubs. Perhaps later the Duke of Edinburgh Award. Can they take part in sports that push them a little – climbing walls at local gyms, river activities, e.g. kayaking and canoeing? There are often open days held locally and supported by the local council or children's services that encourage children and young people to try new things.

Such organisations draw in a cross-section of society, and you must be prepared for this. Parents sometimes want their kids to mix only with children from their own background or area. However, most professionals working with children feel it's good to encourage a wider mix and greater social interaction with children who don't all go to the same school or live in the same area. It helps children to form a broader understanding of society at large and to create a wider and more diverse circle of friends.

Q. *When I tell my B&C child not to do something it's like a red rag to a bull. Five minutes later I find him doing whatever it is I told him not to.*
A. If you have noticed this tendency, then stop saying it and try to think of other ways of getting the point across. While it's very irritating that they are taking no notice, can you think of this in your own context? How would you feel and behave if a work superior was continually telling you not to do something?

Perhaps let them see the consequences of their actions, provided there's no serious threat involved. Talk afterwards about how their behaviour came across and how it would have been seen by others. But do this by asking them for their own observations, rather than by giving yours.

What is it you are asking them not to do? Is it a simple request to alter their behaviour or are you trying to tell them about life and giving them the benefit of your experience to stop them having to go through it all for themselves? If it's the latter, you may have to accept that people don't learn to live their lives by being told – they need to experience for themselves, however annoying this may seem to an observer. Engage your child in conversation, rather than banning things – by doing so you are making it clear that their view-point counts, thereby boosting your relationship.

Q. *My eight-year-old daughter is struggling with friendships at school at the moment. There was a big argument among her group of friends a couple of weeks ago. They said hateful things to each other, and now they seem to keep leaving her out – and making sure that she notices this. I am sure she gave as good as she got, but this exclusion is really hurting her. She wants to be popular and doesn't understand how to get back in with her friends. What can I do to help?*

A. She needs help, and you can assist her by dwelling on the situation with her; thinking about what makes a friend and why. There's an old saying: 'If you want to have a good friend, you have to be a good friend.' Could you help her to think about what makes certain people popular, so she has the potential to understand how friendships work?

When she behaves in a horrible way to others, don't withdraw affection from her. Instead, offer her sympathy and kindness for the rejection she is feeling. Ask what she plans to do. Give her lots of love and empathise for the hard time that she has had.

Encourage her to talk about the difficulties, but then to try to move on and think about how to change things in future. Help her to develop strategies, e.g. to ask friends over or say sorry for what she did but don't make a plan for her – it has to come from her.

If she tries to put things right, praise her for her insight, her braveness and her initiative. And do this even if it doesn't work or backfires in some way.

Try not to see her behaviour as part of you, or to discuss it with the parents of her friends – other than in the most general terms. Giving them specific details which they can pass on to their children, and which then perhaps find their way back to her, will make her feel further betrayed.

9

RESPECT

Preparing Your Child for the World of Sex

CHAPTER SNAPSHOT

This chapter tackles the difficult issue of sex and related emotional and health issues – why it's vital to discuss these with your child, as well as how to approach them, preparing them in the right way.

We will help you to push through any embarrassment you still have, and enable you to talk to your child early and often – so that they can grow up better able to negotiate sexual boundaries. This is important for all children, but especially so for the B&C child.

As we've seen, B&C children are risk-takers. They like to be the first to do everything – particularly if so doing brings them kudos or notoriety with their peers. So it follows that you need to take extra care to talk to them about sex, and to do so well before puberty. You must encourage them to consider choices, risks, responsibilities and consequences – as well as to learn values and respect themselves and others.

A word of encouragement if you still feel daunted: it's not so much what you say that matters, but that you are willing to talk to them – and that they know and understand this. If

they've never yet asked you a question about sex or repro-
duction, it does not mean they don't want to know. The
chances are, they've already learnt this is an embarrassing
area for you and are steering clear.

Why is it so important to talk about sex?

There are plenty of people who lament the trend of sexual
permissiveness among the young, and who think that the
way to reverse it is to keep them in ignorance for as long as
possible. They point back to earlier generations when sex
outside marriage was never mentioned except for occasional
scandals and the sad stories of a few poor pregnant girls who
had to live with the consequences.

However, it doesn't take much to realise that in Western
societies the world has moved on a great deal since then. For
better or worse, sex is no longer the secret it once was.
Young people have a great deal of personal freedom, money
in their pockets and plenty of opportunity for meeting and
socialising with other young people – of both sexes.

Sex is also now much more evident in our daily lives; it's
used to sell everything from magazines and food (or the lack
of it) to floor cleaner and cars. The way people look and
how attractive they are have become multi-million-pound
industries with cosmetic surgery being the new 'must have'
for many.

While a person's sexual behaviour and expression is very
much their own business – and we have no interest in entering into a debate here on what is or is not appropriate – our
concern is for children growing up in a society that uses sex
and sexual imagery quite openly. Children need help to make
sense of all this in a way that enables them to form and
maintain satisfying and intimate relationships in which they

feel loved and secure, and able – should they wish to do so – to raise children of their own when they have reached an appropriate level of maturity and responsibility.

We are sure everybody knows these days that the UK has the highest rate of teenage pregnancy in Europe, as well as worryingly high rates of sexually transmitted infections (particularly chlamydia) among young people. While the reasons for the discrepancies between Britain and other countries are by no means proven, being able to discuss sex and contraception are seen as fundamental tasks in equipping young people in negotiating sex, safer sex or no sex when the opportunity arises.[1]

It is also known that there are certain factors that increase a young person's likelihood of becoming a teen parent. These include socio-economic factors, such as the presence of a father at home, the quality of their relationship with their parents, and the age of their mother at her first pregnancy. For single mothers who had their first child young, and have struggled to make ends meet, being open and clear with their children about sex, relationships and the realities of parenting is even more crucial.

Why don't people talk to their children about sex?

Many parents worry that if they talk to their child when they are young, they will take away their innocence and encourage them to experiment with sex from an early age. There is no evidence to back this up at all and it may well be that the opposite is true – that young people who know relatively little about sex are more likely to find out for themselves.

Another popular belief is the thought that because all schools now teach programmes of Sex and Relationships Education (SRE) parents don't need to deal with it. The danger is that what children learn at school may well be too little, too late for many of them. As part of their survey of schools, the UK Youth Parliament found that 40 per cent of young people thought that SRE in schools was poor or very poor, while a further 33 per cent thought it was average.[2]

So it's your choice. Either leave it to your child's school, and hope it will serve, or make sure that your child gets the SRE you want them to have – including discussions on morality in line with the values and belief systems you would like to pass on. Most people feel more strongly about the latter – but just need some practice in communicating.

Help is at hand.

Why is this preparation so essential for the B&C child?

As we've already discussed, B&C children tend to grow up faster than their peers – at least in their behaviour. So it may follow that they may embark on sexual behaviour earlier than their peers.

There is a tendency for those who feel they are bringing their children up in a comfortable home, with affection and reasoned discipline, to think of teenage sex as belonging to chaotic and poorly functioning families, perhaps also from lower socio-economic groups. They may feel that their own 'well-brought-up' children are not at risk, but children from all backgrounds are just as likely to enter into precocious behaviour, including having sex at an early age.

Because bright and challenging children are clever, they may not necessarily be the ones landed with unwanted pregnancies or choosing to become a younger parent, but they are just as much at risk of emotional damage as any young person. Younger people embarking on sex may, for example, find themselves unable to negotiate the use of a condom, and so put themselves at risk of sexually transmitted infections, which can have life-changing consequences.

So, let's take a more detailed look at why, as a parent, you should get involved in discussing sex with your children, rather than leaving it all to their teachers.

Emotional health and wellbeing

The decision to have sex should be a personal choice, based on a network of personal values and beliefs that guide and support those choices. Casual sex is a choice too – although the decision may be based on a lack of personal values or a mistaken set of popular cultural beliefs.

However, before choosing to have casual sex young people need to understand that all choices have consequences, and the less obvious consequences of casual sex can leave a young person feeling vulnerable and hurt. Some of the consequences you could suggest to your child might include:

- being snubbed by someone they have had sex with feels far worse than being snubbed by someone they have just talked to
- being the subject of gossip
- realising that people want to be involved with them/spend time with them because they have a particular kind of reputation, rather than because of their dazzling personality
- no one wanting to be seen with them
- no respect from partners and friends
- being teased
- feeling jaded and sad about life at a very young age, or even 'burnt out'
- the risk of moving on to something else to derive a sense of fun – something more dangerous

- feeling bad about themselves for choosing to have sex with someone they now dislike or find repulsive

Finding a meaningful relationship in which sex is a progression of intimacy, a way of developing it further and exploring greater emotional commitment and caring, is vastly different – and while it may not always make them feel good about themself, it allows them to have someone to share the feelings with.

Physical risks

The range of physical risks is pretty obvious and it's often these risks that adults feel confident in discussing with young people. They include:

- sexually transmitted infections (STIs) – in younger people some STIs can impact on fertility and sexual health for the future
- unintended pregnancy – no method of contraception is 100 per cent effective
- general sexual health issues such as cystitis or thrush

Cutting childhood short

Young people who become fully sexually active from a young age often miss out on stages in their development. They become too old, too soon.

They may well miss out on the stage of giggling with the girls over people they fancy, or on the play fighting that goes on every time someone they fancy looks their way. Then there's the flirting, being told that someone fancies them and having crushes. Even the joy of a smile or a chance meeting. And who can forget the elation of the first time someone they thought the world of noticing them?

This is all a part of growing up as they hang out with

friendship groups, see relationships developing slowly, go on group dates and explore physicality bit by bit, one new experience at a time.

Experience of sex changes the way your child sees themselves and the way they will relate to other people – so that certain people they meet become potential sexual partners, rather than just friends.

I didn't say anything more but when we got to school instead of just dropping me off my mother pulled into the lot and turned off the ignition. 'Look, Kath . . .' she said, 'I've always been honest with you about sex . . .'
   'I know.'
   'But you have to be sure you can handle the situation before you jump into it . . . sex is a commitment . . . once you're there you can't go back to holding hands.'
   'I know it.'
   'And when you give yourself both mentally and physically . . . well, you're completely vulnerable.'
   'I've heard that before.'

From *Forever* by Judy Blume

We firmly believe that everyone needs to get in touch with their own sexuality before exploring it with other people. Learning how to feel and what is pleasurable is important if a person is going to be able to communicate their sexual wants and needs within a relationship. It takes time, maturity and personal knowledge to gain the confidence to explore one's sexuality with another person fully. Starting too soon can prevent intimacy later on.

Being treated as an outlet for the sexual gratification of another is not good for anyone's self-esteem either, although we accept that in many casual sexual encounters both partners will be seeking gratification from the other, on an equal basis. However, the reality of casual encounters is not always so clear. Many people take years to learn to do so in a way that is emotionally detached. Sex, after all, is intended to stir up our emotions. Like it or not, humans have feelings, thoughts and history.

TOP TIPS FOR TALKING ABOUT SEX

• Take advantage if a relevant situation arises, e.g. a soap opera featuring a pregnant girl, a celebrity pregnant at a young age, tampon ad on television ('Do you know what that is?').
• Get a good book for them to read (or preferably several). But make sure you've had a good look at them yourself first, as there may well be some questions. You might like to read the book with them the first time they read it. That way, you'll know what they have understood and be able to clarify anything that needs it.
• Check out and bookmark some approved websites (see p. 278 for suggestions). You might like to bookmark some for them and some for yourself.
• Listen out for words they use – particularly when they think you are out of earshot – and ask them if they know what they mean. Discourage an overly casual vocabulary if they don't know or understand correct words and terminology. If they persist, read aloud the precise biological definition and ask them if that was really what they intended to say or imply.
• Be aware of the magazines that can be accessed by their age group and ask them questions about content – is it

appropriate for the emphasis to be on the boy enjoying sex more than the girl? We know someone who agreed that her daughter should have a subscription to a magazine she wanted, but only if the magazine stayed in the bathroom for all to read. Be aware too of the 'hidden' sexuality messages – for example, showing very thin models, articles on plastic surgery or breast enlargement in magazines for ten-year-olds.

• Ask simple questions – what kind of things make for a nice boyfriend or girlfriend – kindness, chattiness, friendliness. Explore with them what they consider a good relationship and when they might decide either to stay with the relationship, or to move on.

• Try talking things through on car journeys, preferably when they are on their own – the lack of eye contact and closed environment both helps intimacy and allows them, if things do get uncomfortable, to choose to stare out of the window without embarrassment.

• Talk about issues and topics when they are relevant, as they crop up. Talk one-to-one on some things or as a family for others. Be sensitive to their changing perspectives and development.

• Never, ever tease them about their crushes, feelings or puberty. If you do they may shut you out, and it may be for good.

• Have moral conversations with your child whenever possible. Talk about how choices are made rather than moral judgements, about decision making and taking your time to choose. Don't dictate what should or should not happen (they won't respond to this anyway, because they like to think they know it all).

Sending sexual signals

It's understandable that most kids want the trappings of being grown-up: a bra, a bikini, gelled hair or maybe cool jeans. All children, eventually, want to do things that fit with being grown-up, but the B&C child wants them sooner. They may also be giving off some dangerous messages to the outside world that they may not even understand.

The next time you see a gaggle of schoolgirls out and about in their uniform, or getting on a bus, just take a moment to notice the male attention they draw. While many men take no notice of what are, after all, little more than children, a significant number of all ages will watch them appraisingly. And while some of these young women may be over sixteen, the majority are not. The girls themselves seldom notice the reactions of men outside their own age group. If they are given so much attention when their school uniform clearly illustrates their age, imagine how vulnerable these same young women might be when dressed up for a night out.

The number-one responsibility of a parent is to keep their child safe from harm, as far as they are able. This may mean putting your foot down on occasion, perhaps when your child wants to go to an unsupervised event or to dress in a way that draws too much attention to them. It may cause a row, but, as an adult, you are able to shoulder that discomfort.

The B&C child also tends not to admit that they don't know things – and this can make them even more vulnerable. Rather than look like a foolish child, they will go with the flow, and perhaps end up in situations they can't handle. For example, they can be inclined to act super-confident and worldly, sending out the message 'bring it on' to all and sundry, while their lack of real experience may mean they are quickly out of their depth. An example of how this might happen is on the

Internet. B&C children are likely to flout parental restrictions because they believe they can handle things for themselves. In the process, they may unwittingly find themselves being groomed by adults because they enjoy being treated as older than their years, and they are flattered into believing a potential paedophile's patter and suggestiveness. Most B&C children claim to be very streetwise. Most are not.

Which values?

When it comes to making sound and self-affirming choices about sex and relationships it helps to have a clear framework of values to provide guidance. For example, a child who understands the value of honesty will find it easier to tell the truth to someone close, even in difficult circumstances. It will come naturally to them. Having a framework of clear values does not dictate a B&C child's behaviour, but it can serve to guide them if they choose to let it.

Many parents feel that values are somehow communicated to their children through daily contact. This may be true in some circumstances but maximising the opportunity for children to learn and assimilate clear values can only help the learning process along.

REFLECTION EXERCISE

Here are some values relevant to sex and relationships.

Take a moment to reflect on how you learnt them – which may not be the same as how you were taught them – and, therefore, how you can make them clear to your child.

Adults reflecting on this have said:

I first remember 'thinking for myself' when I used to take the dog out for long walks. I remember the realisation that I could do pretty much as I liked. I could choose which park, which route or path, how long I was away from home (within reason) and how far I went.

To start with, I would follow the set walks I used to do with my mother, but, as time went on, I began exploring more and more. By the time I was twelve or thirteen I would head off for hours at a time. I felt safe when the dog was there, and my parents knew I would never do anything that would jeopardise her safety.

If I relate this back to my son, I guess one way I can help him learn to think for himself is to allow him some more freedom away from me. Perhaps I should get him a dog?

David, father of eleven-year-old Jacob

One of the biggest lessons on loyalty I ever learnt was one time at school when my sister's friend started making fun of me. I expected my sister to stick up for me, but she didn't – she joined in and added some details to the teasing that only she knew. I swore I would never behave like that and I don't think I ever have.

One way I guess I can help my children to learn this lesson is by letting them know what happened to me and how it felt. Also, by showing them that I will never talk them down in front of anyone else even if I'm angry with them.

Eleanor, mother of eight-year-old Zack and
fourteen-year-old Maisie

Values	How did you learn?	How can you help your child to learn?
Thinking for yourself		
Restraint		
Self-respect – caring for one's inner self		
Loyalty		
Consideration for others		
Allowing for the different opinions of others		
Caring		
Trustworthiness		

Feedback

Many people try to teach us the qualities they consider important while we are growing up. We do the same to the next generation. But if we stop to think for a moment about the way we truly learnt these things we might find some surprises.

The biggest lesson Gill ever learnt in relation to trustworthiness was when a friend's mother caught her stealing her daughter's prized crystal bead from her drawer. The shame she felt taught her far more than all the lessons in school or lectures on honesty at home. For her now, when she teaches children about what it means to be trustworthy, she has only to remember the shame that comes from an undeniable inner knowledge of being truly wrong. She has found that when she describes that feeling, many children understand exactly what she means.

So often we try to teach children how to behave well or have principles by telling them what that behaviour should be or what that principle should look like. Sharing stories of things that had a strong impact on us – even if they don't always show us in a good light – help children understand and identify with the issues.

When you can find what truly taught you these lessons, you are in a good position to pass that learning on to your child.

How to talk about sex

Always use the correct biological terms

Example

Eight-year-old Lewis says: 'Girls don't have anything – they just have a hole!'

Possible responses:

'Actually girls have parts of their bodies that are quite similar to boys but they have them on the inside, not on the outside, because they are built to be able to grow a baby on the inside to keep it safe.'

Or,

'The part of their body they have that looks like your penis is called a vagina and it's a very clever part of their body that has lots of muscles. And, just like a penis, it gets bigger when a girl gets excited, but you can't see it because it's on the inside.'

Try to be accurate

Example

Eleven-year-old Natalia says: 'Her trousers were so tight you could see her vagina!'

Possible response:

'I know what you mean, but you can't see a vagina – it's on the inside of her body. The bit that shows on the outside are the labia (in an adult) or vulva.'

If you don't know, look it up

Example

Twelve-year-old Arun asks: 'Is it true you only need one sperm to get pregnant?'

Possible response, after checking it out:

'Well it only takes one sperm to fertilise the egg, but it takes millions of sperm thrashing their "tails" to make it possible for that one sperm to get through the outer coating of the egg. If there aren't enough sperm around, that one wouldn't be able to get through without help – like in a laboratory, for instance.'

Tell them a bit at a time

Example

Seven-year-old Danneka asks: 'What are periods?'

Possible response:

'Periods are something that women and girls have every month when their bodies are mature enough to have a baby. Their bodies store up blood to use in case they get pregnant, and if they don't become pregnant they lose the blood, which comes out of their vagina for a few days.'

Use all topical references

Example

(Mum and nine-year-old Nathan)

MUM: Did you hear about Lorraine next door? You know she was going to have a baby? Well, the baby was born too early, and it was so small it couldn't survive.

NATHAN: Couldn't they put it back until it was bigger?

MUM: Good thinking, but unfortunately it's not possible. The baby was attached to its mum inside and once that connection was broken the baby wasn't getting any oxygen, so it died.'

Check you have made enough of a connection with the information provided before moving on to the next bit

Example

(Mum and eight-year-old Arianne)

MUM: A penis is usually soft but when a man is going to have sex it gets bigger and harder. Why do you think that happens?

ARIANNE: I don't know.

MUM: So that it is easier to push it into the vagina.

ARIANNE: Otherwise it would be too squishy?
MUM: That's right.

Use press stories

Example
(Mum and ten-year-old Connor)
> MUM: Did you see the picture of Angelina Jolie with her twins in the paper? Do you know why some people have twins?
> CONNOR: No.
> MUM: Well, sometimes a woman may release two eggs at the same time, and sometimes an egg that has been fertilised may divide into two; we don't know why that happens, although it frequently runs in families. Sometimes women who really want to get pregnant, and are finding it is taking a long time, may be prescribed a drug that makes releasing two or more eggs at the same time more likely.

If possible get your partner involved so you give both male and female points of view

Example
(Mum to nine-year-old Alice)
> MUM: Well, I know what I thought was important in a boyfriend but let's ask Dad what he thought was important in a girlfriend.

Talk about feelings as the basis of attraction-based relationships

Heart, hormones and head: examine an issue from these three points of view. For example: heart – 'I like him'; hormones – 'I fancy him'; head: 'I know he's trouble.'

Example
(Mum to eleven-year-old Rowan)

Sometimes fancying someone is because you want a boyfriend, and pretty much anyone will do. That's a decision you make with your head only. Other times you feel a real pull towards someone, and being near them can make you start to feel sweaty or sexy – that's a hormones reaction. Your body's chemicals are being switched to 'On' by some of the other person's chemicals! Other times, you just really, really like someone and feel all warm and fuzzy towards them. That's your heart reaction; not literally the blood-pumping organ in your body, but what we call your heart speaking. It means you feel loving towards them and want to be with them. The best kind of attraction is when you have all three – your heart feels fuzzy, your hormones say go for it, and your head says, yes this is a sensible choice for me and I will do well with this person.

Explore relationships from the other sex's point of view

This can help children to understand that the two sexes can have quite different ambitions. Teenage boys can find girls really confusing, and so helping them to understand why girls might want romance and flowers, or the importance of showing a sense of humour – because girls often like boys who make them laugh – can be a real eye-opener. Boys may look disdainful or arrogant, but really appreciate a girl who just chats in a normal way.

Example
Twelve-year-old Rufus's 'girlfriend' has just dumped him to go out with his friend instead; he is angry and hurt, and doesn't see what his friend has that he doesn't.

His mum helps him to work through it, saying, 'Well,

obviously, I think she's mad. I think you are far nicer than Karl, but she must see it differently. What do you think she gets from being with him that she didn't feel she was getting from you?'

Questions and answers

Q. *When clearing out my eleven-year-old son's room recently, I found he had some very explicit sex magazines hidden under his bed. I have always brought him up to respect women, and feel so disappointed in him.*

A. It doesn't mean he was reading them – Alison remembers keeping her mother's old bras in her underwear drawer and pretending they were hers. This could be about keeping face!

However, in reality, it probably means he is curious to know what a woman looks like, and the easiest way to do this is to look at pictures in magazines. And while it may shock you that these images are so exploitative, there aren't really any other ways for a lad of his age to look at images of naked women in intimate detail. Perhaps if there was, he wouldn't choose these.

Don't make a big thing of it unless the magazines are truly depraved. Run-of-the-mill porn is distasteful to most women, but will not cause him to have too distorted a view of the other sex. When the time is right, have a conversation with him about exploitation and sex, just to be sure he understands the issues. You might also want to ask his dad to have a man-to-man chat about keeping his porn hidden in a better place!

For the future, you might also want to warn him about the need to clear out his room and to do it *with* him – rather than embark on it on your own, without notice. It is *his* space, and he has a right to feel safe in it. Right now, he may be more outraged by the idea of you routinely checking his room, without his permission, than embarrassed about what you found.

Q. *My eight-year-old daughter is bright and articulate – and yet in the last six months she has started telling all and sundry that her life's ambition is to be a WAG ['wives and girlfriends' – usually footballers']. I am appalled that she wants to be something so trivial. What can I do?*
A. Well, if this is a way of seeking attention – and if she is trying to shock you and get yours – it has worked hasn't it?

Relax. Very few eight-year-olds actually achieve their early chosen path!

Taking a wider view, it's not uncommon these days for young women and girls to look at the lifestyles of these women and see an attractive alternative to years of hard work, study and regular hours.

But being a WAG has its own issues and difficulties. You might, *playfully*, point out to her that the competition is outrageous, and that you have to be perfectly turned out on all occasions.

Try to suggest a few other female role models to copy – Tanya Byron, Susan Greenfield, or *Blue Peter* presenters (who all look lovely these days). You could also try to give her an understanding that fame does not have to be built on a partner's success, and that she might achieve it in her own right. You don't have to be the sidekick.

As time goes by, and when media stories emerge, you could also try to point out to her the awful reality of being in the public eye day in, day out, what it might be like to have no privacy.

Q. *My twelve-year-old daughter is involved with a fifteen-year-old boy, and recently I found condoms in her drawer at home. I don't know what to do.*

A. Is she having sex or getting ready to have sex? Either way, this is a good place to start a conversation; but it's best started by the kind of question that reinforces her sense of her own responsibility, rather than one that attacks her for making different choices from your expectations or your own experience. Try not to be judgemental or heavy handed – both of which will sound old-fashioned to her.

You could start by saying that you are pleased she is taking her wellbeing seriously, and ask if she knows how to use the condoms. Ask her if she is thinking about this from her point of view, or her boyfriend's (and use his first name because personalising the conversation makes the intimacy of what she is planning more obvious). Explore with her what will happen if she chooses to have sex or if she chooses not to.

Point out to her that she has a whole lifetime to find a partner that she wants to settle down with, and that at twelve, this relationship is unlikely to last long.

Be kind, *really* listen to her answers and try with all your might to leave your emotions out of it as you explore hers.

The bottom line is that she will follow the course of action that she chooses, but she may not have considered all the options; or, perhaps she is making a 'head' decision (see p. 205) based on pressure from her boyfriend.

Encourage her to seek advice if she is in any way unsure and help her to find a local young person's sexual health counsellor or a trusted and confidential other adult (such as an aunt or older cousin, or even a sister) who can help her through.

Gill has met a parent who, in similar circumstances, sat her daughter and her boyfriend down and asked for a frank discussion. The daughter was undaunted, but the boyfriend was so embarrassed and tongue-tied it pretty much ended the relationship anyway.

Q. *My ten-year-old son has always preferred the company and playthings of girls, and now he is approaching his teens this looks set to continue. I am seriously worried that he may be gay. How do I stop this?*
A. You can't. He is what he is and has a right to be. If he has always been like this, how would a conversation with you change his mind?

Right now, he may well be dealing with the same difficult issue you are acknowledging, but at only ten will feel vastly more insecure. Try to reassure him that he is loved and cared for, and to ensure his sense of self-esteem is maintained. Whatever his sexuality, he is your beloved son. If he is indeed gay he will need to be supported in a world that can be prejudicial and cruel, so don't add to it by making it harder for him. Love him for who he is and be glad you have him as he is because his sexuality is a part of his whole being and not just an add-on.

If he needs help understanding his sexuality as he gets older, try to find someone he can talk to or look up a young gay and lesbian group where he can make friends. Don't push him, though; he may well be straight but enjoy girly things – there are plenty of camp straight men out there.

[1] *Teenage pregnancy: an overview of the research evidence*, Teenage Pregnancy Unit, Health Development Agency, 2004
[2] UKYP, *SRE are you getting it?* June 2007

10

WASTED

Preparing Your Child for the World of Drugs and Alcohol

CHAPTER SNAPSHOT

In this chapter we'll be exploring the issues around drugs and alcohol. The B&C child, we know, is particularly keen to be seen as grown-up and may well see sex, alcohol and drugs as clear markers of their development into a young adult.

As parents, you need to think about how you can prepare your children to make healthy choices as they get older, and restrict them long enough to keep them safe – until they have a clearer view of the issues involved.

What kinds of drugs should you worry about?

Parents often worry about illegal drugs, but alcohol remains by far the most readily available of all drugs, and potentially the most dangerous, both to indulge in and to be around when others are using it. So many accidents, acts of violence, sexual assaults and crime involve alcohol in some way, and it is by far the largest single co-factor in most teenage pregnancies.

Many people believe that the classification of a drug in law gives an indication of how 'dangerous' it is to an individual. This is not so. A leading police officer told Gill a while ago that if alcohol were invented today it would be a class A drug, along with heroin and crack cocaine. However, as it is almost impossible to do otherwise, it remains legal.

The legal drugs – smoking and drinking

In past generations, girls wore shorter skirts than women, boys wore shorter trousers than men, and there were clear markers to demonstrate the passage from childhood to adulthood.

Today, however, fashion starts at birth, and even newborns can have denim jeans and baseball caps – nor is it unusual for girls under ten to have make-up, bikinis and high heels. Children in primary school talk about their boyfriends and girlfriends and dress like teens, listen to the same music as teens and talk like teens. While they remain very much children in terms of their maturity and vulnerability, they embrace anything that shows them as more grown-up than they are.

Because, as a society, we have largely done away with 'rites of passage' from childhood to adulthood, with the exception of those for whom faith and adherence to it are central to their lives, such as many Moslems and Jews. In such societies children study to become adults by learning the laws of their faith and exhibiting their knowledge as an important marker of maturity. But in the wider society, there is nothing official; kids now make their own markers to highlight their transformation from childhood to young adulthood.

When I have conversations with seven- and eight-year-olds about the difference between being a child and being an adult, by far the most commonly mentioned difference that they see is that when you are a child people tell you what to do, and when you are an adult they don't. So it's no wonder that our bright and challenging children are so unwilling to be told what they should do.

As children get older, by about the age of ten or eleven, they begin to add 'going out' and in particular 'partying' to the list of things they aspire to do as young adults, as well as 'taking exams'. By the time they are aged about eleven to thirteen and are at secondary school, they are beginning to add activities to the list that have been marked in law as for adults only – smoking, alcohol and sex.

Gill

SOME INTERESTING STATISTICS

By no means all children try smoking or will drink alcohol unsupervised. Statistics show that the number of children from eleven to fifteen trying cigarettes in England has dropped quite considerably.

A 2006 survey found that 9 per cent of eleven- to fifteen-year-olds claimed to be regular smokers, with girls at 10 per cent and boys at 7 per cent,[1] but the statistics for 2007 show a fall to 6 per cent.[2]

The 2007 statistics for alcohol show that 20 per cent of pupils in England aged eleven to fifteen reported drinking alcohol in the week prior to the survey being conducted. Among eleven- to thirteen-year-olds the number of young people drinking has gone down, from 14 per cent in 2001 to 9 per cent in 2006. However, the amount consumed by eleven- to thirteen-year-olds increased from 5.6 units a week to 10.1 units in the same time period.[3]

While we can be pleased to see the downward trend in these figures, the fact that almost one in ten eleven- to thirteen-year-olds reports regularly drinking (and the amount they are consuming) is alarming. Of course, we don't know how many of these are having a small glass of wine at the dinner table, but our guess is not many.

For many young people, legally restricting things by age acts as red rag that attracts, rather than signalling something to avoid. For B&C children, the list of prohibited items becomes a checklist, bringing attention in return for indulgence in what is forbidden.

Children may see smoking and drinking as part of growing up and this attitude is frequently reinforced by parents who smoke or drink in front of their children with the statement 'not till you're older', 'it's OK for adults' or something similar. Many children of smoking parents are aware of the age that parent was when they had their first cigarette. This is a story they may well have shared more than once. Probably they intended this to be a cautionary lesson for their child but for the B&C child it is a target to be beaten.

While restrictions on smoking are undoubtedly helping to reduce numbers of smokers and the frequency and quantity of cigarettes smoked, this applies mostly to adults. Young people smoke in parks or open spaces not bars and restaurants. They smoke in the street or in the homes of peers with unrestrictive parents.

Up until the age of around ten to thirteen, most children think smoking is dreadful and swear they will never do it. However, they often seem to go through a change of heart, and many of the most vociferous begin smoking themselves. A higher proportion of B&C children choose to smoke and often start at a younger age. The reasons they start are varied but among the most common are:

- They grew up around smoking or still have a parent who smokes
- They have been challenged by other young people to smoke, and are not prepared to risk being seen as a wimp or a child
- They see an association between smoking and being an outsider or rebel

Dealing with these issues requires different directions for parents. If you smoke, or have a partner who smokes, there is a very high chance that your child will too. Stop for your sake and theirs before they reach that 'turnaround' age. As a reformed smoker, you'll no doubt eventually find cigarettes disgusting and smelly – share your changing views with your child. And let them see how hard it is to give up.

If yours is a child who is likely to be at risk of behaviours that they have been challenged to participate in, work with them to be more assertive and independent. Help them to realise that the true maverick is the one who dares to challenge even the minority viewpoint. If they see themselves as a rebel, or would like to be seen by others as such, try to make them see that certain behaviours are actually the markers of the 'sheep' in society, rather than the movers and shakers.

As with so much in parenting, the best practice is not to give a one-off 'lecture'; you need to plant seeds, then water them through discussion and questions, drawing your child's attention to situations around them and reflecting on attitudes and opinions.

As for drinking, parents who laugh at their child's first sips of alcohol and who tease and encourage them to try different drinks can hardly be surprised if they find out their child is regularly drinking from a young age. Family attitude to alcohol is key in helping children to develop an inner moral code around it. If drunkenness is seen as funny and excessive consumption of alcohol lauded, there is a chance that these are the attitudes that will be passed to the child.

More subtle messages come from parents for whom the arrival of visitors or certain occasions are always accompanied by alcohol. Or those who get home from work and immediately pour a glass of wine or a gin and tonic. They are passing on a clear message to their children that alcohol is essential both to have a good time and relax.

We know that bright and challenging children will always be more at risk of anything potentially damaging because they are headstrong and independent way too soon. They are also intelligent enough to work out ways of getting their hands on anything they want, regardless of legal restrictions. Gill has even met a twelve-year-old who made his own alcohol, and she has been asked for details of how alcohol is made when talking to children in primary schools.

B&C children whose physical maturity allows them to get around restrictions will turn this to their advantage, while others use charm and quick thinking to persuade otherwise upright members of society to help them, whether it's the corner-shop owner or the lady next door.

Example

Twelve-year-olds Emma and Breanna were close friends from early childhood. Breanna is a girl who would fit our profile of a bright and challenging child. They both became members of a group of mainly fourteen- and fifteen-year-olds by being able to regularly supply the group with cider. Breanna had made friends with the young man who worked in the local mini market who would serve her when no one else was around. He realised she was too young to be buying alcohol but didn't realise how young she was.

Both Emma and Breanna were affected negatively by their association with the group and began to identify more and more with these out-of-control young people. Emma started to miss school to go drinking in the park during the afternoon and began engaging in a range of sexual behaviours with some of the group members. Breanna's mother eventually traced the source of her daughter's drinking and complained to the police that her daughter was being sold alcohol under age.

Breanna stopped meeting with the group after her mother's interference, possibly because she was embarrassed or perhaps she was no longer amused without the alcohol. She and Emma eventually drifted apart and their friendship ended.

It is probably true that teaching children about sensible drinking from an early age helps them understand and get used to alcohol. The French have always allowed their children to drink watered-down wine at the dinner table and have nothing like the teen alcohol issues we see in Britain. Some might say this is because the children are learning good drinking habits and this may be true, but it is also significant that being seen openly drunk in public in France is regarded as both shameful and socially inappropriate, unlike in Britain. They don't have the heavy drinking and partying culture there that British youngsters have. Britain is seen as the 'badly behaved drunk' capital of the world, which is precisely why drinking has such an appeal for the young – anything goes.

Many parents allow a child small quantities of alcohol as they get older, and may even supply them with alcohol at parties, etc. However, remember that children don't drink like adults. Given an alcoholic drink, most youngsters will down it in as few gulps as possible, which, in itself, is dangerous, as it gives them no time to assess their competence levels before choosing to drink again or not.

Once, when I had friends to dinner I bought a large bottle of ready-prepared Buck's Fizz for the two thirteen-year-old girls who were coming, having checked with their parents before the evening to see that they didn't mind them drinking it. I introduced the girls to each other and pointed out to them the range of non-alcoholic drinks available and 'their' bottle of Buck's Fizz. Within five minutes they had finished the whole bottle, chugging it down in large water glasses. While it contained very little alcohol, the amount it did have went very swiftly to their heads and they giggled away for an hour before becoming dopey and bad-tempered. The fault was entirely mine, for allowing them to help themselves rather than giving them a small glass every hour or so throughout the evening.

Gill

The best way to help your B&C child learn to treat alcohol with some caution is by encouraging them to understand from a young age that alcohol changes elements of the personality, putting people in danger of acting foolishly and riskily (but not cleverly or funnily). This will help them to take a more wary view of alcohol – because if there is one thing that the B&C child hates, it is to look foolish. It is probably a good idea to point out that another consequence of too much alcohol is throwing up – something that is unpleasant, smelly and definitely 'uncool'. While being incredibly drunk and acting wild may enhance a B&C child's reputation with their peers, being uncontrollably sick and pathetic certainly won't. If you can bring these aspects of alcohol to their attention, rather than the bravado and excess of bragging to peers, in the longer term you may be helping them to make better and more self-supporting choices.

The illegal drugs

Cannabis

By far the most commonly used of the illegal drugs at any age is cannabis. In 2005 1 per cent of eleven-year-olds reported using cannabis, with this figure rising to 27 per cent for fifteen-year-olds.[4]

Cannabis is sometimes seen as the 'next step' from tobacco as they are usually smoked in the same way. For many, this is another step towards being grown-up and being seen as a risk-taker by their peers.

Most young people will come into contact with cannabis users from a young age. It is widely available and in most secondary schools pupils will know who can get cannabis for them, or who regularly smokes and sells it. The majority of sellers will be young people either buying for their friends or to reduce their costs in buying for themselves (they buy twice as much as they want and sell the rest on at a slightly higher cost). Where these young people get their supplies from varies, but it's often a family member, such as an older sibling or uncle who sees no harm in cannabis and encourages its use. While legally a young person 'selling on' cannabis to their friends is 'dealing', most parents see dealers as unscrupulous individuals making money out of the naïvety of children, rather than class- or schoolmates. The reality of how the drug is most usually obtained may surprise them.

Parents sometimes find it shocking to realise that their pre-teen children know anything about illegal drugs, let alone much more than they do. Many parents consider drugs to be part of the cultural 'dark side' along with knives and crime, and can be appalled to hear their children refer casually to drug taking, and with a vocabulary that sounds so informed.

The term 'drugs' can be quite misleading when used in the media, as it covers a huge range of not only different substances with differing properties, but also different patterns of use – from those of high-flying executives to festival-goers; doctors, teachers and lawyers to people living on the street; parents and neighbours to gun-toting gang members. It's important to understand that a lot of the harm caused to society by drugs comes as a result of the fact that the drugs are illegal rather than from the drugs themselves. Prohibition in the US is often cited as the start of organised crime, and certainly the formal ban on alcohol, and the desire among the population to continue supply, allowed mob crime to flourish. Today, those who make a living out of buying and selling drugs – and particularly those who aim to get rich doing so – have no protection in law for their business dealings, so they create their own way of ensuring 'respect' from others, often involving intimidation, violence and extreme acts of retribution.

To adults, all the negative reports in the press and the criminal activity we may experience as victims adds up to something to be afraid of; to children and young people, they simply represent the far edges of something ordinary, in the same way that stories of people who are so fat they cannot get out of bed represent the far edge of overeating, and the guy pushing the shopping trolley shouting at everyone in the bus station represents the far edge of drinking alcohol.

A lot of children grow up with parents who regularly smoke cannabis, often in front of them or when they are in the house. While they are young, they may well not notice but as their awareness grows, and their drug education becomes more detailed, they will begin to understand what is going on. In such circumstances, it is hard to tell children about the negatives of drug use in a way that is convincing, and parents may shy away from it all together.

Many parents will not have a problem with cannabis use, and may even consider it harmless and acceptable. We certainly know of cases where children smoke cannabis openly in the home, and of parents who ask their children to buy cannabis for them. And some people argue that using cannabis in front of children encourages them to use it sensibly, in much the same way that drinking alcohol with them encourages sensible drinking.

In recent years, however, a lot of new information has become available about cannabis and its particular impact on the developing teenage brain; for major brain restructuring takes place at this time. There are strong links between cannabis use and mental illness during adolescence, and the long-term effects of cannabis on the developing brain are still not fully researched or understood. It should also be noted that the cannabis around today is often a lot stronger than that which parents may have smoked in their youth and, therefore, potentially more harmful.

One thing we do know about cannabis is that it affects the short-term memory, and this is a good starting point for a discussion with your bright and challenging child: smoking cannabis makes them forgetful – in other words, their highly prized intellect will be impaired. While cannabis can make people sit around and contemplate the meaning of life or the problems of society, heavy cannabis users are frequently rather inarticulate and have problems thinking things through rationally. Fortunately, these side effects are generally reversible, except in cases of very heavy and protracted use. But would a B&C child want to do something that meant losing their fantastic verbal skills, risked permanent damage to their mental health and compromised their ability to reason?

Other drugs
It is rare to find a child between the ages of eight and twelve using illegal drugs other than cannabis, although they may get access to other drugs if they have money and a lot of freedom. And this is one of the reasons why you need to keep a tight rein on the B&C child as they grow older. Too much freedom too young can lead to dangerous experiments.

Cocaine, Ecstacy, LSD and ketamine are all widely used by young people, particularly on the club and dance scene. Most children will not have access to these for some years beyond the scope of this book, but there is a very small minority for whom it is surprisingly easy to get into places that should be keeping them out. It can be very difficult to tell the age of a young person these days (Gill has frequently met children in year six who are taller than her, and she is average height for a woman), particularly girls, who may use make-up to look older. Some very young people certainly do get into clubs using false ID, but the majority of precocious behaviour will be at private parties, friends' houses or in public places such as parks or high-street areas.

Many young people assume that something you smoke is less dangerous than anything you might swallow, and under-thirteens are generally quite wary of taking pills or snorting powders. So they are less likely to use Ecstacy or cocaine, but they are also more willing to try drugs that are smoked – probably because they have already tried or are regularly smoking. The connection they fail to make is that heroin can just as easily be smoked in a cigarette as injected – but it is still heroin.

Gill once talked to a thirteen-year-old who had been smoking something she thought was cannabis, but which was almost certainly heroin. She was too concerned about her image to ask too many questions from the person offering it to her, and assumed that if it was smoked it must be cannabis.

Why do young people take drugs?

There are many possible answers to this question. By far the most common one given by adults is 'peer pressure', while for young people it is 'fun'! Try the exercise below – it might help you find some answers for yourself.

REFLECTION EXERCISE

Four simple questions (answer them as honestly and as fully as you can):

1. When was the last time you took a drug?
2. Which drugs have you taken since this time last week – and how many or how much. Why did you take each one?
3. How many famous people can you name that have been known to use an illegal drug?
4. How many TV programmes have you heard make reference to drugs in the last month?

Feedback

If you have been honest, a new insight into why young people take drugs may have been gained.

Young people take drugs because we all take them. We live in a drug-taking society where just about everything from alcoholism to exam anxiety can be treated with a pill. In simpler times, headaches were treated by lying down in a darkened room or having a sleep; tiredness was treated by sleeping; too much energy was dealt with by doing something physical; and a nasty cough was sorted with lots of hot, soothing drinks. Today, we don't have the time to let our bodies recover in this way – we have drugs to do the job instead.

Children grow up with the notion that how you feel – both physically and emotionally – can be 'fixed' with drugs. Recreational drug use, including illegal drug use, is merely an extension of this idea. It's common to read in the papers that a young person (usually someone who had come to no good through the experience) had taken 'a cocktail of drugs', and parents may assume this means a random selection, taken all at the same time. In fact, their use is generally much more considered than this, and the 'cocktail' referred to might better be described as 'mixing their drinks'. Many young people on a night out will take a mixture of drugs for their effects at different stages of the night. So they may start with a drug that enhances sociability when they first meet their friends, then move on to a club and take a different drug to boost energy and appreciation of music for dancing, then later on take something to help them relax and sleep.

We also live in a society where many of the role models for young people are known to be drug users, and many more are assumed to be, even if their use has never hit the headlines. We're not implying that young people use drugs just because their favourite band or celeb uses them, rather that taking drugs is not seen as anything detrimental or undesirable. Famous and successful people are known to use them (though not that many intellectuals or scientists, perhaps) and come to no harm. Their careers are often meteoric, regardless of drugs, so those messages adults give about drugs messing you up are clearly not true in all cases. Drugs are a significant part of popular culture. They are as influential to young people as sport, music, fashion, communication, and so on. They are part of what defines and shapes today's identity for whole sections of young people.

So, how should you talk to your children about drugs and alcohol?

Many parents find it difficult to talk to their children about drugs and alcohol, so they either ignore the subjects completely, or simply say: 'Drugs are bad. They kill you. So don't ever use them.'

To any child this is pretty unhelpful. They will soon learn that they don't kill you and their peers and cool older kids certainly don't think they're bad. And it's those cool older kids who get heard – not you.

When your child is five, your word is law to them (although they may break it all the same); by the time they are eight or nine, their peers' opinions are becoming quite important to them too, although they still generally consider you to know best; but once they reach twelve or thirteen (and you can knock that down by a year or two for a B&C child) for most parents, your days in the sun are over. Children will look to their peers for role models, approval, answers and guidance.

To a B&C child the 'Just say no' approach is often counterproductive. For this child, more than any other young person, your disapproval triggers a little note to self: 'Hmm, interesting!' Everything that is on the fringes of acceptable behaviour will be of interest to them, and many will consider it essential to try all of it in the interest of exploring who and what they are as they get older.

Approach drugs with the B&C child in much the same way as you do everything else. Engage their intellect and encourage them to form opinions of their own. You do this by asking them what they know and what they think, from as young an age as possible. Use stories in the news or soap-opera storylines to involve them in a non-personal dialogue:

- Why do you think (a famous singer) takes so many drugs when it's affecting their performance/ appearance?
- Why are so many celebrities going into rehab all the time?
- Is it right that famous people can break the law on drugs and not get arrested?
- Why do so many famous people take drugs/drink too much?
- Why do so many footballers seem to get into problems with alcohol?

B&C children like to be asked their opinion and it's vital to listen to them rather than argue with them. By all means, make points for them to consider, but bear in mind they may well take up an opposing or shocking viewpoint from yours in order to be seen as radical or non-conformist, and the more sensible points you raise, the more theirs may become fanciful and extreme.

A ten-year-old once gleefully proclaimed to Gill that he felt it would be a good idea if everybody went away for two weeks to a sort of holiday camp where you could try every drug available, under medical supervision, so that you knew what they did to you and which were either suited to you or potentially harmful. From then on, you could use the ones you liked. She told him she thought he had obviously thought carefully about how to reduce the risks associated with experimenting with drugs and had made a good suggestion for that type of drug use. What he had not yet considered, however, was how to reduce the risks associated with regular or long-term use, the varying strength and quality of street drugs and, of course, the other great variable – how other people may behave towards you when you are under the influence of a substance. He nodded wisely.

Talking to children about long-term effects has little impact. Most have no concept of meaningful life after forty, and will often answer, 'Good, I don't want to get old anyway', when told that they risk dying.

Highlighting the altered appearance of those who are regular smokers or drinkers is a good way to get your child to consider alcohol and smoking, as most young people are very interested in how they look or how they present themselves to others.

You can also try quoting other people, to show that smoking is neither glamorous nor attractive. Features in the paper showing faces ravaged by addiction are good discussion material, as are some extracts from books. Alison read a passage by Stephen King to her children about his mother dying of cancer (Stephen King, as a horror author and creator of *Carrie*, counts as cool!):

Dave woke me at 6.15 in the morning, calling softly through the door that he thought she was going. When I got into the master bedroom he was sitting beside her on the bed and holding a Kool for her to smoke. This she did between harsh gasps for breath. She was only semi-conscious, her eyes going from Dave to me and then back to Dave again. I sat next to Dave, took the cigarette, and held it to her mouth. Her lips stretched out to clamp on the filter. Beside her bed, reflected over and over again in a cluster of glasses, was an early bound galley of *Carrie*. Aunt Ethelyn had read it to her aloud a month or so before she died.

Mom's eyes went from Dave to me, Dave to me, Dave to me. She had gone from one hundred and sixty pounds to about ninety. Her skin was yellow and so tightly stretched that she looked like one of those mummies they parade through the streets of Mexico on the Day of the Dead. We took turns holding the cigarette for her, and when it was down to the filter, I put it out.

On Writing: A Memoir, Stephen King

TOP TIPS FOR HELPING YOUR CHILD STAY DRUG-FREE FOR AS LONG AS POSSIBLE

• Encourage children to see the use of drugs as sad rather than glamorous. Drugs stop us from being who we are, and are mostly used by those who do not take pride in being themselves and who want to lose part of their self-consciousness.

This approach will ring bells with the B&C child, who is enormously proud of themselves, yet, paradoxically, has poor self-esteem. They may think they're marvellous, but they also know they make mistakes and hate themselves for doing so. It follows that getting them to focus on the aspects of drug use that diminish their glory, rather than prop up their ailing and weak side, will help them to create a negative attitude to drug use.

While they may change their mind once they reach adolescence, this will, at least, give them longer to mature and to become capable of making decisions.

• Help them to think about how to live healthy lives from a young age and praise them for making healthy choices, healthy suggestions and expressing healthy attitudes.

• Encourage them to have strong views about the world and the behaviour of people in the limelight.

• Get them to take into account the lifestyle of individuals they choose as role models, and to be discerning.

• Don't show approval by laughing at drunken behaviour.

• Think about your own alcohol use, and be aware of the messages you might be giving.

• Don't smoke; show distaste at the smell of smoke and smoking.

• Get your child to consider the crime and suffering that is associated with drugs and how these affect people's lives. Everyone who uses an illegal drug is encouraging this crime to continue. (The Taliban are one of the major groups to benefit from growing opium for heroin production.)

• Be informed about drugs yourself – perhaps with your child's help. Search the Internet and read up on drugs and their history, their effects, their methods of use and risks.

• Above all, avoid preaching. It's far more effective to engage your child in discussion and reasoning. If, at the same time, you make it clear to them that the choice will ultimately rest with them, and that you trust them to make sensible decisions, it sharpens their sense of prestige and responsibility. If possible, enlist the help of a sensible older sibling to discuss what is appropriate and what is not. (For tips on introducing healthier rites of passage, see Chapter 7.)

Questions and answers

Q. *I am sure that our eleven-year-old son is sneaking alcohol from our supply. I can't prove it, but the bottles have definitely gone down and I am sure it is him. What should I do?*
A. Talk to him about it. Not in an accusatory way, but to let him know that you have noticed, you are concerned and wondering what to do. If there are no other people living in your home then this becomes a bit obvious, but if there are others around then try to keep the conversation open. This may act as a deterrent in its own right – or he may get smart and start topping the levels up with water. Unless you have huge stocks and they are going down at a risky rate, don't lock it away or hide it, but don't replenish the stocks either. Get all your children to help you and watch out. Make it a problem to be sorted as a family rather than an investigation into a crime.

If the amount being taken is extreme, seek medical help – drinking at such a young age on a regular basis can cause long-term liver and heart damage.

Q. *My ex-husband is an alcoholic and this was the cause of our relationship breaking up. He left when my son was eight (he is now ten), but I am worried he's learnt from seeing his father drink and will think that this is 'what men do'. How do I counteract this impression?*
A. You need to talk to him about his father's drinking and how it was a problem. Perhaps you could explain this as a reason for your break-up, but not with blame or discredit. Simply discuss how excessive alcohol use makes it difficult for people to connect with each other.

You could ask him if he understands what alcohol is and what it means in terms of behaviour, relationships and dependency. People who are dependent on alcohol are not good at intimacy and at coping with life. If you get him to notice these things, perhaps he can appreciate what drink does to someone. Give him an opportunity to talk about how he sees his father, drunk and sober. Many children of alcoholic fathers actually associate their fathers' drunken behaviour with being fun and charming, and their behaviour when sober with being depressed and miserable. It is also common for children of alcoholics to see their sober parent as the 'spoilsport'. You will have to unpick any of these attitudes with him, as they can influence his future behaviour.

Talking to him in this way may make him feel quite uncomfortable initially, but will also show that he has been trusted with important information and that you are prepared to talk to him honestly about adult issues.

Q. *We both smoke and want to make sure our children do not.*
A. Simple. Give up now and try to involve them in the process, so they can see just how hard it is to do. You owe it to yourselves and your children to do this. It will be hard, but given the anti-tobacco education they receive at school they can help you.

Q. *My ten-year-old daughter jokingly said, during a conversation about an ultra-skinny singer with a much publicised heroin and crack addiction, that she would take heroin when she gets older to make her skinny too. I know she wasn't serious, and was just being smart to get a reaction from everyone present, but ever since I have felt quite uneasy. Should I talk to her about it and risk making it a big thing, or let it go and assume she'll forget about it?*
A. She may have been showing off a bit with her comment, but it shows that somewhere along the way she has internalised that extreme drug use = very thin. Hopefully, your daughter will find a hundred ways to shine in a crowd in

healthy and successful ways, but adolescence can shake up even the most well-adjusted child to behave in extreme ways. I think you should talk to her about it, not in terms of your worry and concern, but to ask her if she understands why and how the drug use of this singer has led to her weight loss. It isn't simply that heroin makes you thin, rather that extreme heroin use means the user stops feeling or experiencing normal physical and emotional cues to care for themselves. The weight loss, while potentially dangerous in itself, is also a sign of a more dangerous lack of care about basic survival. And rather than just concentrating on the weight, get her to consider other aspects of the behaviour of this individual – why she is using the drugs she does and what they are doing to her emotionally, professionally and physically.

[1] NHS, Statistics on Smoking: England 2007 [NS]
[2] NHS, Statistics on Drug use, smoking and drinking among young people in England in 2007
[3] NHS Statistics on Alcohol: England 2007
[4] NHS Statistics on Young People and Drug Misuse: England 2006

11

'ALL I CAN BE'

Values for Life

CHAPTER SNAPSHOT

One of the most noticeable changes in parenting over the last twenty years has been the attitude that children should grow into their own person with their own skills, abilities and beliefs. As a result, we are seeing a big difference in the way children and young people behave.

On the positive side, there are numerous exceptionally confident young people who are using their gifts to further their own lives in ways that support and nurture others. The flip side, however, is that there are also more young people who take no responsibility for their own behaviour or choices. There is more asserting of power using violence and the threat of violence, a worrying increase in alcohol consumption and its after effects, less social responsibility and more 'me, me, me' behaviour.

This chapter does not intend to tell you what you should be telling your B&C child about life and the big issues of society. Rather, it provides a brief outline of some of the values we believe B&C children should be introduced to if they are to become viable members of both a community and wider society.

Who is providing your child's values?

As many of the values that we live by are put in place very early, the most influential people in a child's life are undoubtedly their parents and carers. They teach the young child to care about others, to look after themselves, that they are precious and special, but also that the feelings of those around them are to be respected and nurtured too.

While parents are influential, it is worth pointing out that what you do is so much more influential than what you say. A smoker who tells their child not to smoke because smoking is bad for them will usually find that child becomes a smoker too.

Gill recently met a child whose smoker mother had offered each of her three children a thousand pounds if they had not smoked by the time they were eighteen. The two eldest lost out (they began smoking by twelve or thirteen), while the youngest, at ten, was looking forward to his cash bonus. She saw this as a real symbol of modern parenting: offering material incentives to make up for not giving a child what they really need – a sound set of values and good role models.

Today, parental guidance is not a given. Even the most fundamental of lessons is missing in the lives of many children: perhaps through lack of time or inclination; perhaps through a belief that the next generation should make up their own minds, rather than being told or taught what to do or how to behave.

Other adults provide a learning opportunity for values. Family and friends, childcare providers and schools all play their part. As we have become more and more sensitive to the diversity in our evolving society, there has been a 'backing away' from adults who are involved in childcare in relation to providing any kind of opinion or viewpoint about the world in front of children, in case something is said that may offend or counteract the view of a parent. While this is a laudable development in many ways, there needs to be an acceptance of certain core values that are not related to any particular group, religion or political affiliation.

Parents of children with childminders or nannies might speak to their child's care provider to ensure that they are able to provide some basic framework of values for their child and, to avoid mixed messages, that these values are the same as the parents'. Schools also need to think about the values they embody and how these are presented to children in uncontroversial and meaningful ways.

As they get older, children will be increasingly influenced by peers, including some who have not had a sound grounding in values from early childhood. This is sometimes a positive and desirable outcome and sometimes a disastrous one: the vacuum you provided to let your child have the space to make up their own mind may be filled by others with more demanding views. A child with sound values is more likely to find friends with values similar to their own; a child with little sense of values risks being attracted to extreme or power-based behaviour in others.

B&C children, being even more demanding than most, may see themselves at the centre of family life from very early on. When they demand, entertain or act out, everyone laughs, appeases, explains or drops whatever they are doing to give the all-important attention that drives the child. As a result, they often grow up with an admiring circle, rather than understanding the impact their behaviour has on others.

B&C children are also more often leaders than followers. As such, they will frequently operate in the extreme end of the accepted-behaviour spectrum. Put such a child in with academics and studious children, and they will often become the most studious; put them in with a faith group, and they may well become a fanatic; put them in with a socially responsible group, and they will become champions of the underdog in all spheres. Realistically, the B&C child will be in an environment where all of these possibilities exist. But whom they choose to lead will be influenced by where they see themselves as most likely to be noticed and whose opinions matter most to them.

The mean screen

One of the worrying influences on young children and their values framework is computer games. This is the first generation of children who have grown up from birth with a range of computer games and supporting special effects. Even small babies can now have a 'toy' computer and mobile phone, as well as interactive games. In many computer games, the main aim is destroying or killing. In computer graphics on TV, and in film, disaster and wholesale destruction on a mega-scale are everywhere. Children absorb information like a sponge when they are small and no one can really say what all these images do to their view of the world. It's not unreasonable to assume, however, that playing games where repeatedly killing nameless two-dimensional characters, or destroying cars or planes over and over again, might lead a child without other guidance or influence to have little regard for life.

Within limits, computer games and images are probably not damaging: as long as the child has learnt to distinguish reality from play, has developed empathy and compassion and knows how to recognise and manage their feelings appropriately. If they haven't, then perhaps such games can feed anti-social or aggressive tendencies and serve to isolate a child in a world where they can decide the fate of everyone they meet, and deliver devastation and mayhem, at the push of a button.

Television, of course, is a huge source of values for us all and for children in particular. What they watch and how they interpret the things they watch are important. The programmes that a family watches together also act as a shared value and how they watch is crucial. Consider the soap opera. What values are demonstrated by an average storyline? It's usual to find drug misuse, alcohol as a social necessity (they nearly all seem to revolve around a pub), adultery, marriage break-ups, single-parent families, violence (or the threat of it), deception and betrayal. In days gone by, the stories to which children were exposed nearly always had moralistic outcomes. Today, the literature for children and most TV designed for children alone will still have clear consequences for poor behaviour. Adult TV or film, however, has quite a different structure. Popular programmes that may seem harmless and even educational can impact quite dramatically on children. Hospital dramas can make them anxious about their health, cop shows can make them anxious about crime and violence, 'shoot 'em ups' can lead them to see life as disposable (in others). In days gone by, a serious illness in someone close did not happen often, but when it did it became a major talking point; for the hospital drama viewer it is a weekly occurrence. Serious crime and murder affected the lives of relatively few people, now they happen in our living rooms almost every day. TV itself is not harmful. Children can learn a great deal from what they see on TV – even from soap operas, but it is how they view and the way in which they process what they see that is crucial.

Community

The groups or communities to which a child's family belong will also influence their values as they grow. Children raised in a faith household will be exposed to a set of shared values that will often last a lifetime, even if they choose not to adhere to the faith they were raised with. While for many parents it is their own experience of being raised within a faith that has made them determined to leave their children as blank canvases, it is possible to raise a child within a faith to still consider options and choices and to be open to other influences. Being raised within a faith community does not have to mean indoctrination if the child is taught to understand the diversity of belief around them and to be allowed to make up their own mind about their beliefs. The only real risk for the B&C child is that they may become fanatical or extreme in any belief they live with as a way of standing out from the crowd. They may also choose to break away from any faith held by their community as a way of inviting attention.

Other communities that a child may be influenced by in terms of values can be subtle and hard to define. In some communities, taking anything you can get is the accepted norm – if it isn't screwed down, it's fair game. In others, keeping yourself to yourself is paramount – no matter who asks for anything or seems in need.

Here is an exercise to help both you and your child focus on the values they are learning and have right now.

REFLECTION EXERCISE

Ask your B&C child these questions. Try not to add too much information – simply ask the questions as they are written even if the child wants more detail.

Money

Where does money come from?
Is money important?
What happens if someone doesn't have any money?
What do people need money for?

What values did they express?

Relationships

Is it more important that you like your friends or that they like you?
If a friend hurts or upsets you what would you do?
What does it mean when someone says 'sorry'?
What do people like about you?

What values did they express?

Violence

When is it OK to hurt someone?
When is it OK for someone to hurt you?
Why do so many people carry knives?
Is it ever OK for someone to kill another person?

What values did they express?

Community

What should happen when someone is old and lonely?
When should you say thank you to a stranger?
What are the 'rules' about how to behave in public – such as on a bus, in a café, walking in the street?
What is the job of the police?

What values did they express?

Feedback

When I asked my ten-year-old son where money came from, he confidently replied 'the bank'. I wanted to query this, but I let it be and asked him the rest of the questions. He said that money is very important because people judge you on how much you have, that if you don't have any you can't buy 'stuff' and you end up on the street.

His reasons for why money matters so much were all to do with impressing people, including 'the best-looking girls' and buying things he wanted. There was no recognition of meeting needs and certainly no awareness of rent or bills! I was quite shocked really; I think I had a far greater understanding of money and what it meant when I was his age.

                                   Father of ten-year-old William

I asked my twins about violence. What was amazing to me was how different their answers were and how they were pretty typical of the views of boys and girls. My daughter was all 'violence is wrong', while my son was full of 'if they deserve it or if they start something'. When I asked about killing someone, my daughter felt there might be justifiable circum-stances – maybe if they were going to kill you or if they had already killed someone. My son said, 'If you're at war with them.' When I asked him what that meant, he told me that anyone can be at war with anyone else – even neighbours can be at war with each other. So I said does that mean a neighbour can kill another neighbour and he looked a bit concerned but then said, 'Yes, if it's serious enough.' I was horrified.

                   Mother of twelve-year-old twins Lucinda and Michael

What principles should you be passing on?

The following list is a basic one we have drawn up to provide some guidance. The values we have chosen are based on humanist principles, rather than forming part of any particular religious or political persuasion: they are about learning to be accepting, tolerant and living together in a community.

1. Life is of fundamental importance to all

Everyone has a right to life and no one has the right to take it away. Just because someone does something you don't like, this does not give you the right to take away their life – no matter how upset you are.

Hurting and harming others is wrong, regardless of how much you, at times, may feel they deserve it. The young today hear from their peers (and sometimes their parents) a message of retaliation and retribution, in particular when insufficient 'respect' has been shown, but this can lead to bullying, exclusion and hurt. The right to life is fundamental.

The B&C child may have strong feelings about who should be 'allowed' to live and who should not.

Example
Nine-year-old Denholm is watching the news when an item about overcrowding in British prisons comes on. After a couple of minutes he disdainfully announces that he doesn't understand what all the fuss is about and that in his opinion all criminals should be killed. This, he says, would make sure that people were a lot more respectful of the law and would save a lot of money and time while solving the overcrowding situation.

His mother pointed out that crime was varied and did he think that not paying taxes, getting in a fight or driving while drunk all constituted grounds for death? He was adamant that he felt that they all did.

His mother then pointed out to him that she had herself in some small ways undoubtedly broken the law on occasion – such as speeding perhaps or dropping litter. She asked him if he felt that meant she should be killed.

He thought about it for a moment and then said, 'Yes, then you would have learnt not to do it again!'

While it would seem that Denholm has yet to fully understand the nature of death and its permanence, his callousness to others who are not himself is concerning in a nine-year-old.'

2. Allowing difference

People and things can be different; not everyone needs to do things in the same way. So it's acceptable to have different religions, colours, ethnicities, customs and beliefs, and to make different choices. Accepting diversity enables you to see difference as just that – simply different. Neither better nor worse, and therefore not something to mock, laugh or deride. Remember that the way you behave is far more powerful than anything you say; your responses will be copied.

Everyone has equal value or worth, and even if an individual is exceptionally good at something it does not make them more valuable as a person; just better at the thing that they do.

Bright and challenging children can be xenophobic and prejudicial, wanting the whole world to be the way they want it to be and adhering to their views (and worshipping them of course).

3. Self-reliance and personal responsibility

This is about taking responsibility for yourself and your actions, drawing the line of accountability back to yourself and what you did to affect a situation. Understanding choices for yourself and how the choices you make may impinge on other people's rights. For example, playing music out loud on a bus takes away the right of others to silence; playing music with headphones allows everyone to have what they want. It also involves accepting that everyone has to do things to make their lives work and no one else can be blamed if things don't work out as they may wish.

B&C children only want the spotlight to highlight the areas in which they shine. In general, children who are attention-seeking revel in any attention at all, be it good or bad. They would rather be shouted at than ignored. However, the B&C child, by definition, is only interested in situations where they get the glory – they are the number one. It can happen, of course, that what the child is trying to achieve is to be the number-one 'wind-up', or the number-one cynic. When situations are uncomfortable for them, they will shift blame and responsibility to anyone they can. Even to you for having them in the first place.

Example
Her school has sent eleven-year-old Honey home for wearing a non-uniform skirt for the third time in a week. When her mother questions her about why she has not worn one of her two uniform skirts she replies, 'It's not my fault, it's a stupid rule anyway.'

4. Everyone has feelings – they just express them differently

Everyone has feelings and even if people are unable to express them effectively, they still have them. It should never be assumed that just because someone can't be articulate about how they feel, their emotions do not matter or can be downgraded.

It's arrogant to assume that our feelings are more significant than those of others or that we have 'deeper' or more sensitive feelings than them. Culture, upbringing, shock and verbal ability in English can all affect how easily someone might express how they feel, but the expression in no way reflects the feeling. It is safest to assume that in any given circumstance an individual will have the same depth of feeling as we might have in the same situation.

We regularly come across examples in the media where the belief that people ought to behave in a certain way leads to a public assumption of involvement, guilt or complicity in wrongdoing. Mothers whose children have gone missing being required to weep publicly, or the royal family not being seen to be openly mourning after the death of Princess Diana are examples. There is a common opinion that in areas of the world where child mortality is high, parents don't feel pain 'as we might' because they expect it or are used to it. Pictures of exhausted and shocked disaster survivors' blank faces as they hold their dead and battered children are cited as proof that 'we' feel things more intensely. Interestingly, there would be a public outcry if a news bulletin featured a British mother holding the battered body of her child, who had just died in a road accident, in front of the cameras!

B&C children may feel that they have more intense feelings than anyone else, and as their empathy skills can be poor (until it suits them to allow them to be greater) they seldom consider the feelings of others. For example, if they cause hurt to others, they will try to convince anyone who will listen that, in fact, the greatest hurt is theirs, as they have to deal with the resulting criticism.

5. Relationships and society as a whole involve give and take

This includes the fundamental truth that relationships require an element of investment from everyone involved if they are to work. B&C children get a lot back from others when young because they are articulate and demanding, and inclined to sulk or act out if not given what they want. As they grow older, they may have to learn the hard way that these tactics no longer work. Also, the tricks that work with their family and schoolmates may not work in a world where no one *has* to put up with it. The same is true when we extend individual relationships to encompass society as a whole. Expecting to be taken care of and forgiven all transgressions will change as an individual gets older. All children must understand that if society is to work, we all need to contribute not just expect to get something back.

6. Receiving attention is not the same thing as being liked

There has never been such a fame-hungry generation. Partly, this is because fame is seen as a route to money and a golden lifestyle, but also because it is seen as being 'loved' by the world.

Very young children equate attention with affection. Babies, in particular, relate to eye contact as a marker of affection and care before they can even speak or understand words. So most children seek attention from adults to feel loved and secure. As they grow, this stretches and words take on an increasingly important role along with the actions of others, facial expression and body language. Some children get stuck into a need for attention to such a degree that any attention will do even if it is negative attention – being shouted at is better than being ignored.

All children should understand that attention without approval is not a route to happiness. They may be getting what they want in the short term, but not long-term respect or liking from others. One of the greatest risks for the B&C child is social exclusion. They are often not popular once their novelty and youth have worn off. A thirty-year-old behaving like a precocious four-year-old will be pitied, ridiculed or excluded in most circles.

B&C children need to learn to value and maintain loving relationships as if they were learning a foreign language – step by step and in detail. They will have a lot of hurt if they don't learn that being appreciated by an audience is not the same as being loved for who you are.

CASE STUDY

Ten-year-old Cameron was always very bright for his age. He walked early, talked early and was always the centre of attention when in adult company for being unusually opinionated for a young child. His parents frequently held discussions with him about all sorts of items from the news and current events, encouraging him from the age of four to express his opinions.

When he attended family gatherings he was always made a great fuss of with adult after adult seeking him out to ask his opinions. These were mostly childish and a source of amusement to many of the adults. His parents dressed him in adult-style clothing which accentuated his oddness. He frequently wore suits and bow ties even to birthday parties when other children would be wearing jeans and T-shirts.

He had little in common with other children but seemed happy in adult company. By the time he was six most of the children in his class ignored him. By the time he was eight most children in his class ridiculed him. As a small child he was hailed as a prodigy or at the very least an oddity – an eccentric. As he grew older he seemed less brilliant and more of an odd-ball to everyone. However, he was used to being the centre of attention and had no strategies for commanding attention within his peer group.

When he was nine he started to tell lies to his classmates as a way of getting them to notice him or listen to him. These lies often involved famous people or wealth and possessions. For example, he told the children in his class that he had been given a Porsche car by an uncle. As he was only nine and could not drive on public roads this car was being kept for him at his uncle's house in the country where he was allowed to drive it at weekends.

To start with some of the children believed the stories but as they became more and more extravagant it became apparent to everyone that they were simply not true.

Rather than admit his fantasising or changing his behaviour, Cameron began to make the stories even bigger and harder for the children to dispute. It became apparent to everyone that Cameron was in need of help when he told his classmates that his father had won millions on the lottery. They were sworn to secrecy with promises of money and gifts. Cameron began giving children IOUs for hundreds of pounds.

The school contacted his parents who were horrified at his behaviour (and potential irresponsibility in handing out prom-ises of money). By working together his parents and the school developed a programme of social skills for him which provided him with both the attention he craved from adults and ways of getting appropriate attention from his peers.

7. Family and close relationships matter

Our close relationships really count and children must be encouraged to maintain them. When a child is young their family will tolerate them even if they are badly behaved and selfish, but in the long term, relationships are up to an individual and they need to maintain and build them. Even a family can get lost in time. Many ageing parents hardly see their grown-up children and grandchildren, while many adults have little or no regular contact with siblings.

There are times when we all need others. When bonds are maintained, the people you can always rely on to be there for you are your family. They may not always like each other, but families have a shared bond that, if maintained, lasts a lifetime. What supports that bond is a shared understanding of the importance of give and take, and not just receiving. As people grow older, they tend to keep close contact with people who have proved their reliability and commitment during tough times. The people who are there for us when we need them are usually those we are there for when they are in need. Effort is required in keeping relationships going, in particular when things get tough and people fall out with each other or circumstances cause hurt or upset to one or all family members. Children should grow up understanding the importance of discussing what went wrong, celebrating good times, allowing for different opinions and views, giving praise and congratulations to others when earned, giving up on personal preferences in favour of the communal good and allowing everyone their turn in the spotlight.

Having learnt these skills and beliefs within a family, it is easier to transfer the understanding to other relationships that they may form in life. It is too easy today to throw away things that are broken – including relationships. Learning how to mend things that are broken still matters.

In a wider sphere, understanding that no one is an island is a fine principle and value to promote. We are all inter-connected and interdependent, even if it is not apparent, and this is true globally. What affects one country or community will affect us all.

B&C children, with their strong belief in their own infal-libility, may not see the need for maintaining relationships with their family and may have no close friends. By talking to them about the role these people play in your life, you can help them understand the long-term importance of such relationships.

8. Money alone doesn't make you happy

Money and things don't necessarily make you happy, though we accept that the lack of it most certainly can make you unhappy. Material goods and the acquisition of them may give a short-term buzz, but this is lost almost the moment the packaging is opened or the new item is taken home.

Young people often view what you have as being a fun-damental part of who you are. There is an equation in their thinking between material goods and a person's 'worth' as a human being. They are encouraged to want by the media and lifestyle advertising, friends and popular culture.

If a person has no money or material possessions, it does not mean they have no value. Modern society has invented a range of indicators of value that are meaningless in any real terms such as the car a person drives, where they spend their holidays, what 'labels' they own and where they shop. Alison remembers hearing comedian Lucy Porter's shocked response to a new boyfriend who told her that, on principle, he 'did not date renters' and discussed her children's equally shocked response with them. Hearing strong opinions from parents and those they look up to can distort the values of children: they pick up from us what we value and how we see ourselves and those around us.

Gill recently worked intensely with a group of fifteen ten-year-olds. The children were being trained as 'peer mediators' and about half of them would probably be classed as 'bright and challenging' by their school if the question had been asked. As an introductory activity, she invited them to work in groups to devise a list of ten questions to ask her that would help them to know as much about her as possible in a short time. The groups were mixed boys and girls. Along with a few questions about her favourite colour, food, sweets and television programme, they asked her:

- what countries she has been to
- what her house is like
- what her road is like
- which make of car she drives
- which shops she shops at and her favourite shop
- which supermarket she favours
- how many televisions she has in her home
- how many holidays she has been on

No one thought to ask her about the things she cared about, how she spent her time, her interests or beliefs. No one even asked about her work or her family.

B&C children are not necessarily more materialistic than other children, they are just *more anything*. If football rules in your family, they will care more than anyone else; if you are a family of foodies, they will be avid viewers of all food programmes and love to eat out in restaurants; if money and material goods matter to their peer group (and they tend to), they will be label hounds who attach great value to what they have.

How to develop values in children

The best way to develop positive values is in the way you live, and how you demonstrate your own values. This will have a huge impact on children. So you have to be careful about what you say in front of them – 'not in front of the children' is a bit old-fashioned, but a good principle.

B&C children are precocious and will carefully listen to adults in conversation with other adults. They will then use what they learn, so as to seem more mature and grown-up to their peers. There are times when it is not appropriate for them to hear what you are talking about.

So if you fall out with a friend, or have an argument with a family member, it's a good idea to talk to them about the reconciliation, how you managed it (in an exploratory, rather than triumphal spirit) and how you feel about it. All too often, children hear about what went wrong in adult relationships as you let off steam within their hearing (if not directly to them), but they are not around to see the make-up.

Discussing conflicts seen on television, and how they can best be resolved, can be a less exposing way of doing the same thing. Ask their opinion about what should be done or thought – and give feedback for their wise and considered point of view.

It's fine to state your beliefs about any issue if you have them and have thought things through, but you have to be aware that others may see things differently and need to be allowed the same freedom. Allow your child to disagree if they wish and let go of the adult desire (or is it a childish one?) to always have the last word.

Many parents listening to a child will add some comment like, 'Well, you might think that now, but you'll see when you grow up.' While it may be true that their opinions will change, such a comment dismisses their opinion as childish. Let them understand as a general principle that our ideas and thoughts about things change as we grow older and have greater experience, but they don't all end up the same. Having thought-through opinions, however naïve they may seem to you, is a positive and laudable trait, as long as they accept that different people will have different opinions, and that all opinions are equally valid to the person holding them.

Listen to their opinions; encourage your child to have them and praise them for being able to express those views. Then try to extend their thinking. If you say they are wrong, put them down or mock them, they will not tell you again.

Notice and reward them when they demonstrate positive values – when they take care, show kindness or empathy to others, even if you have asked them to, but especially if you haven't. Comment on this/make it clear you have noticed. Discuss values with them and their importance to a good life for the self and others.

Keep a close eye on what they are watching and absorbing on television and ensure that they aren't watching stuff that's inappropriate – for example, programmes that are overly violent, aggressive, uncaring or malicious. Because B&C children are precocious and both seem and act older than their years, it can be tempting to allow them to watch programming or films designed for older children or adults and to interact with them while watching in a way that is inappropriate for their age. Gill recently had a conversation with a ten-year-old girl who had watched a documentary about a child born with eight limbs as she was joined at the torso to a parasitic twin. The programme was graphic and she asked the child what she had thought of it. She replied that she thought the mother of the child should have aborted her daughter before birth and that she would have done so in her place. Failing that, she would have given the child 'to a home' rather than looked after her.

In a different setting, this ten-year-old girl could have had a very different reaction to this programme. She could have been encouraged to marvel at the care of the doctors who managed to operate on the baby to remove her twin and to restore much of her normal body function; she could have empathised with the parents of the baby who were torn between leaving her as she was and putting her through gruelling surgery; or she could have understood how lucky she was, as an able-bodied child in a caring home with free medical care and a loving family to support her through her early life. Whatever the conversation was that took place during the programme we can only guess, but an opportunity to extend the values of empathy and gratitude were not taken up.

It can be difficult to know what children are picking up from what they watch and it may be something very different from what you think. Watch with them – in this way Alison found out that *My Super Sweet Sixteen* – a fly-on-the-wall reality show about a party being organised for a spoilt sixteen-year-old – was, in fact, being watched with irony and amazement, rather than as an exultation of conspicuous expenditure.

As a general rule, don't allow your child unsupervised access to TV or DVD, however tempting a bit of peace may be. Pretty much every childhood behaviour guru has now come out publicly to say that allowing a television in a child's bedroom is a bad idea. We add our voices to theirs.

Children's stories have a very moral basis and tend to make values very clear. Use stories and books that are age-appropriate; reading with and to children is a great shared activity and one that reinforces good morals and generally good behaviour too. There may be a fair bit of violence in *Harry Potter* but there are also love, friendship, good versus evil, care for the underdog, empathy, friendship, the importance of family, sound role models and nobility of thought and action as desirable qualities. Even the more anarchic children's writers like Roald Dahl always shows good being rewarded and evil not. The stories of Jacqueline Wilson reinforce the principle that whatever awful things happen to you in life, whether through accidents of birth or subsequent misfortune, love, kindness and friendship can ensure that people work through difficulties to lead fulfilled lives. All good stuff.

Mealtimes make the perfect platform for discussion, as do family evenings with no TV, running over forthcoming events and sorting out family issues.

On one of Gill's recent workshops about B&C children a parent stated that she had no intention of giving her child any values – she wanted her son to develop his own, uninfluenced by his mother or any other adults. This may seem a fine idea but children are not blank canvases and will not sit long and hard pondering the universe before deciding what values to live by. All children will be bombarded by messages from a range of sources and the B&C child will probably pick these up faster than their peers – after all they pick up everything else faster too.

By definition B&C children are rather self-centred individuals, at least when they are young, who do not always put the greater good above their own. They need to learn that they will be happier if those around them are happy too and that what makes others happy is a shared viewpoint and understanding – a social glue. While we want all children to shine, we need them to do so in ways that allow everyone else to love and respect them.

Questions and answers

Q. *My son's best friend is always playing war games and has a selection of guns and other toy armaments that I consider very unsuitable. My son is entranced by the things he has and wants to play with them – and him – all the time.*
A. What you must not do is to say he can't play with his friend or his friend's toys. Whatever you ban becomes even more interesting, as I'm sure you know. The illicit feels good and banning or rationing makes them even keener to play.

It is a common and normal thing for a child to have a fascination with toys that go bang, or pretend to, and if he has had none of his own he will be all the more eager to play with these strange new things.

Overall, are you being a bit precious? If the toys are age appropriate, is there really a problem? Children will make guns out of Lego or even a stick and pretend to shoot with them.

The important thing here is not the toys themselves. Children can play harmlessly with anything and all play is valuable to a child's development; particularly imaginative play. What matters is that your son understands some difficult ideas and has a sound understanding of the value of human life. He needs to appreciate for himself why guns cause you to feel alarmed and to be able to recognise the difference between playing with a toy gun and playing with a real one – that real guns do terrible things to people and that once shot, most people do not get up again! We were told by one young person that when he saw someone who had been shot, he was appalled by the devastation and damage it caused the victim. It wasn't a neat bullet hole that left a bit of a red stain on the victim's jumper!

He also has to understand the place of guns in the world –

their use in hunting, the military and in different places in the world – as well as the damage they cause to individuals, families, societies and even nations when used inappropriately.

All of this sounds so dull, but we're not suggesting a lecture. What needs to happen is a series of dialogues about guns and weapons over time, even a few years, to ensure that your son's fascination with the toys don't lead to a fascination with the real thing or the people who use them (except in a controlled environment).

Q. *I heard my daughter expressing extreme sexist views recently and did not know how to respond.*
A. Was she doing this to shock you perhaps? If you are really concerned, ask her to talk about it some more and gauge what was really behind what she said. You might have got the wrong end of the stick.

However, it could be that this is what she thinks, in which case some greater discussion and exploration of viewpoints will be needed as she grows older.

It's possible she said what she did to fit in with her friends; if so, she may need to be reassured that it's possible to be friends with people you don't agree with, as long as you don't feel obliged to take on their views. The other possibility is that what she said is a reflection of her views and those of her friends. You cannot change the views of the friends but you can work with your daughter to see the world differently. If you limit her access to people you agree with, you are being as dictatorial and intolerant as the viewpoints she is expressing. Children can see all kinds of values around them and this does not mean they have to agree with them.

Q. *My child is arrogant. Those he sees with fewer possessions or less able than him, he is inclined to dismiss or see as beneath himself.*

A. You need to reinforce the sense of value of others – as equally valid people in the world, with others who love and care for them. Demonstrate to him how *you* value others and include them in your life and thinking. Work with him to see that it is not only those with status or valued things who have value. People with nothing are still somebody's son or daughter and have an intrinsic value, and everyone contributes to the world in some way.

Your son is very insecure about his own worth as a person and so seeks to make up a way of putting himself in the top category. He is worryingly competitive and needs to learn that value is not only about academic achievement – or any achievement in the eyes of others necessarily, or getting more money. He has to understand the qualities that society values in others and to strive towards developing himself towards such goals. (See also Chapter 6.)

Q. *My partner and I have totally different political views, something that we found interesting when we first met, but we are worried now about the very mixed messages our children are likely to absorb. What can we do, when neither of us wants to change our minds?*
A. It's a good idea to show respect for each other's values – whether political, religious, moral or dietary. For instance, explain how they work and try to stress the common ground – in your case that you both feel strongly about how society should be ordered and what the government should try to achieve.

The good thing is that your children are likely to grow up *more* tolerant through understanding two different points of view, so strongly held. They will appreciate that there is not just one solution for the good ordering of life, and that will help them think about their own responses. Have some good family discussions and enjoy your differences as a family.

12

LOOKING TO THE FUTURE

We wrote this book to support the parents of children aged eight to twelve, so this chapter is designed to provide some things to think about for the years that follow.

One of the main issues with B&C children is that they are inclined to be very self-confident and so tend not to want as much contact with their parents as their less confident siblings or peers. As they hit adolescence, you will find they want even less contact with you as they begin to establish some real independence – and you need to prepare for this.

For those who want to look at this in more detail, there is a whole book on the subject of adolescence – *Whatever! A Down-to-earth Guide to Parenting Teenagers* (written by us) which you may find helpful. But in the meantime, here are some tips.

Continuing support for your B&C child

1. The big change

The approach we have been advocating throughout this book has been less negotiation and more parental setting of boundaries – and firmness in implementing them. This will have to change as your child grows into a teenager. They will need to be allowed more negotiation and freedom. But if you have been following the advice in this book, you should be able to relax the boundaries a little from a position of strength, rather than starting from having none at all.

It's been your responsibility as parents, with more life experience, and an understanding of cause and effect and financial responsibility, to keep your child safe and make decisions. Now they will want more freedom and responsibility themselves, and you have to think about how to pass the baton on.

In future, you will probably have to adopt a model of shared decision making, and if you have found this a difficult line to hold in the past, you are going to find it even harder in the future, as hormone levels change dramatically – probably for both parties.

2. Allow them more freedom as they show more responsibility

B&C children genuinely believe they are capable of looking after themselves in any or all situations well before they really are. Reining them in is sometimes hard, unless you have already got a good system of boundaries in place. In which case, the trick is to allow them more responsibility and freedom when they can show they can handle it. So you might need to devise some steps between where they are now and where they want to be, and see how they do at each stage. If they mess up, then it's back to the drawing board. Make this process clear to them too, so that they feel in control of the changes that are taking place in their lives and feel neither hemmed in nor pushed out – two things that these children are prone to feel. They also need to know that the process of change relies on them not *telling* you how mature they are, but *showing* you. This requires a degree of trust on both sides – but only as far as the next step.

So if your child wants to be allowed to go to the nearby major town centre alone on Saturdays, the first step might be to go with friends, for them to call home at intervals during the day, and then be back at a stated time. If they manage this a couple of times with no hitches, the next step may be that they can go without needing to call in, though still maintaining their curfew. If they slip up, get home late, forget to call, etc. they go back a stage for a while which, in this instance, would either be not going into town without an adult or calling throughout the day.

They will not approve or agree if they have to be taken back a stage, but as long as they understand the process and the way in which you are allowing or disallowing things, they will have some control over it.

Be upfront about it all – nothing creates more tension than adding new rules halfway through a process and none of us responds well when the goalposts seem to keep moving. Let them know how things are and will be, well before it becomes an issue. Of course, this is easier for second or later children and harder for eldest or only children, as you might not yet know what needs to be considered.

3. Keep communication going at a time when they seem to want it less and less

If you have previously enjoyed a close and loving – even if at times tempestuous – relationship with your B&C child, the advent of the teenage years can be a shock, as they may no longer seek to communicate unless they want something. Parents can find themselves having to try ever harder to communicate before they make decisions. Most parents have some understanding of how it feels to be a teen (after all they were one themselves once) and want to ease their child through the process as quickly and painlessly as possible. It can therefore seem hard when the child you are trying to do your best for won't talk to you about the issues you are trying to make decisions about.

One of the least effective ways of communicating is to fire questions at them. They simply clam up or grunt. The most successful approach is probably to maintain those habitual moments of intimacy from their childhood as they get older. If you have always had your meals together in the evening, make an effort to maintain this. If you have shared friendly shopping trips to the supermarket with chats as they help you load and pack away, maintain them, even though it might be quicker and easier to do them on your own or online. If you have a shared love of football or a favourite sitcom, keep watching together, even if their perspective on the entertainment and your relationship changes dramatically. Those shared times will provide the perfect opportunity for talking about all or nothing as time passes.

You must accept too that interest in you and your shared life will wane as they seek new challenges, away from home. As they become more able to use public transport and bikes they will no longer need you to drive them around quite so much either. While you may have moaned about all the time this took, it's easy to feel displaced and this can hurt.

4. Help them to develop friendships that don't involve you

At primary school, even the most outspoken child is tolerated. While they are young, their peers and the adults they come into contact with find a novelty and entertainment value in them. They may, however, find it more difficult at secondary school where their idiosyncrasies and selfishness may result in them being left out by virtue of numbers – there are now hundreds of potential friends for each child, and they no longer have to get along with everybody in the same way. B&C children may find themselves teased, isolated or called names. They may also find that teachers and other pupils don't like them. The harder they try to impress and stand out, the less popular they may become. Where once they were remarkable, they are now annoying, odd, irritating or just plain different and they might well find the power of peer pressure working against them. They may need emotional support and some kind tips to help them find and maintain new relationships.

Many B&C children don't have good friendships, and need help in making new ones and keeping the ones they have. One way to help them might be to talk through your own friendships and how you overcome issues of boredom and conflict.

Watching television together can help. Many programmes or films designed for young adults feature friendship issues at their core. However, the B&C child can be disdainful of watching anything too mainstream, so think creatively!

5. Learn to accept that they are separate

B&C children at their best can be dazzling and the centre of attention at home. Living with one means that parents and family always have something to talk about. There are always anecdotes, concerns, funny stories and deeds or misdeeds to be shared; emotions will be stimulated, conversation will be generated and problems will be aired.

If they are an only child either by birth, or because older siblings have moved out, they can completely dominate the family – and so their adolescent desire to be away from it as much as possible can be difficult. When they are no longer around, or are taking themselves away for most of their active time, it can seem that there is nothing to talk about. This is true, to some extent, of all children but is specifically so of the B&C child. When you do see them, they can be uncommunicative and diffident. As mentioned above, it is vital to keep communication channels open so that both parties can talk when necessary, and so that neither forgets how to.

However, you should also begin to develop a new relationship with other family members and partners that does not centre around this child and their behaviour. They may find this quite threatening as they see you begin to have your own private life again, but you must find a balance if you are to let them grow up successfully into an independent person.

6. Promote independence

Independence is both a state of mind and a series of skills – those we often refer to as 'life skills'. All young people have to learn a variety of skills as they grow older in order to manage their own lives. These range from simple mechanical skills, like using an iron, to more complex skills, such as managing money.

B&C children are not easy to teach (ask any teacher). They are quick learners, but they tend to try and run before they can walk. They are the kind of people who never read the manual – no matter how unfamiliar the territory they find themselves in. Neither are they good at the 'look and learn' approach, preferring to jump in head first and have a go at anything new. Then, if all goes well they reap the praise, and if things go badly, they will find someone or something else to blame.

So, while you should teach them your wealth of wisdom, this must be done so that they can learn in their distinctive way. Never tease them for their failures, never over explain and never underestimate them. So tell them that from now on they are responsible for all their own ironing and every time you see them in something that looks half decent praise it to the hilt. Enrol them in a family *Apprentice*-style competition to make the most money over a six-month period (if you can afford to) or to see who can source the weekly shop for the cheapest bill, while maintaining the quality of what is bought. Such tasks will whet the appetite of many a B&C child – though not all, of course. While preparing your child for their adult lives, remember at all times that while this can be difficult, and their skill with words often means that endless negotiation is needed, they are still a child. However confident they seem, they don't necessarily have the skills to back things up and supervision and monitoring still make a difference.

7. Financial independence

One of the big changes that has taken place over the last couple of generations is the amount of money young people are given to spend – the so-called 'teen pound'. Parents have more money than their own parents had, and, fuelled by strong memories of how it was to go without, tend to be more generous with their own children. They also give in to pressure from both their children and the media. We often hear parents bemoan the state of the world where they simply cannot deny their child the latest video games console 'as all the other children have them and he/she will feel left out'. Anyone with any sense knows this is simply not true. No wonder so many parents talk about how bad their children are with money, and no wonder so many young people hanker after the lifestyles of the rich and famous where unlimited money is spent on every whim.

Help your potentially reckless B&C child to become responsible with money by encouraging them to earn it themselves, understanding its value and what it buys. At the same time, don't overburden them with material goods – wanting things provides motivation. Show them how to save up for things because, in the long term, they will value them more. This sounds quite old-fashioned, but is profoundly true. Increase their sense of value and pleasure in owning by making them wait. Then, when they finally have a much longed-for item, they will often realise that its value lies not in its cost in terms of money, but in terms of the effort required to attain or achieve it.

As they get older, by all means give them an allowance with which they can buy a clearly defined range of things. Be careful to specify what is included in the allowance and what isn't – such as college stationery or tampons. Try letting them budget for everyone and involving them in making family decisions, such as new furnishings or a family holiday. Involve them at all stages and allow them to understand the process of budgeting – this will give them a real sense of achievement.

8. Teaching self-motivation and personal management – the importance of planning ahead and thinking about the future

B&C children are easily bored by the mundane and by repetition. They love new experiences and can be thrill-seeking, so it's important to provide them with the skills they need to keep on doing new things and get involved. If not, they may risk more damaging choices of behaviour, as we have explored.

Remember that they tend to get bored easily so can be quick to give up; boost their motivation and encourage them to stick with things. B&C children are not natural team players and not good at being long-term, goal-orientated people. They want instant gratification.

Help your child to find things that interest them, new challenges, risk-taking in a safe environment. Be aware that this may take you into areas you have never thought about before and which may not appeal to you right now.

You will also have to accept that you don't share some of the personality characteristics that they show, while trying not to feel personally undermined by this either. For example, it can be hard to be seen in public with someone dressed head to toe in black, or to be in a theatre with someone who uses the interval to deliver a loud and highly critical view on all deficiencies of the leading actor, but it is them and not you who is making these choices. Help them manage their energies and accept that they are show-offs, while encouraging them to also think of others.

Don't give up – however tempting! When your child reaches the age when childcare is no longer legally required, you may feel that it's time to ease off and take more time for yourself. Alas, not so – parenting teenagers takes time.

THINGS THE BRIGHT AND CHALLENGING CHILD MIGHT LIKE TO BE INVOLVED IN

- Amateur dramatics/music – they tend to like things where they can show off and fulfil their desire to be watched
- Debating clubs
- Political societies – most have youth sections
- Starting a society of their own (Gill ran a charity to help save Abu Simbel temple; Alison set up a roller-skating club)
- Science – museums and workshops

- Poetry and writing clubs that admit junior members
- Writing competitions in libraries or magazines
- Setting up a junior branch of a charity and organising a fund-raising event (and inviting the local paper along to take pictures)
- Organising a family party or treat; researching what everyone would like to do and then designing and sending out invitations
- Decorating their own room or planning for the shared use of space with a sibling; arranging enough storage and being clear about whose is what
- Work experience with someone you know in a field they are interested in
- Setting up an enterprise (for example, a babysitting or local waitressing and washing-up service)
- Physical activity, joining a club or taking on a personal challenge (e.g. a long sponsored bike ride)
- Entering competitions
- Compiling scrapbooks reflecting on what they have done
- Sorting through their stuff and putting it into relevant storage boxes; deciding what to keep and what to throw away
- Designing a website or helping someone organise Facebook pages
- Writing a blog
- Writing a book or short stories

The aim of all this is to keep your child busy and motivated, so they are not tempted to pursue other ways to get attention, such as self-harm or excessive alcohol use.

Developing your antennae for when your child is lying

B&C children are verbally able and inclined to be manipulative – and so we tend to believe them. They have learnt not only how to use words well, but also those tell-tale non-verbal clues too. They are often masters in body as well as spoken language. Bear in mind that they will say or do pretty much anything in order to get their own way, and that they may be neither honest nor straightforward with you.

Most parents believe that their child is essentially honest with them and that while they might exaggerate or omit facts occasionally, they will not tell out-and-out lies. When they want something badly enough, most young people will push for it, but the B&C child usually has no scruples in doing or saying to anyone what will best serve their own purpose. In general, they are not routine liars, but they are perfectly happy to fob you off with whatever you want to hear if it serves them to do so. As far as they are concerned, they're doing it for you – to stop you worrying or getting upset or because you can't handle the truth. So they may well tell you they are going to a friend's house when they are, in fact, going to an all-night party.

The bright and challenging child really knows how to manage their parents and to spin a yarn. What they tell you may have an element of truth in it somewhere; they know that all good lies are based on truths, so that they can provide some back-up if required. Small children tend not to lie because they feel their parents always know the truth, but as B&C children get older, they get better at telling stories, and early successes will urge them on to other lies.

It's a good idea to get into the habit of double-checking; be wary of assuming that what they say is the whole picture.

They may then factor in the possibility that you may check into what they say. Many parents are aghast at the idea of not trusting their children, but if your child is aware that you may double-check, it encourages them to tell the truth. Try not to make the checks seem as if you doubt them, rather make them part of your parenting routine. So if your child is staying over at a friend's house, phone in advance to thank the friend's parents for their kindness, or buy them a small present which you know will be acknowledged when you next meet. If you always do this, your child will think twice about lying to you in future.

Look to help and support for you

Parenting teenagers can be exhausting – all the more so if you have children of different ages or are a single parent – and the urge to get out of their lives and leave them to it can sometimes be enormous. They say that parenting is a lifelong occupation, and although it gets easier once they have reached adulthood, it never stops altogether.

As your child gets older, you should develop friendships with people you can empathise with and who can empathise with you. Maybe you can do this through your child's school or maybe through other affiliations, such as parenting support or book groups.

Make extra effort to take care of your own relationships. In particular, it's a good idea to discuss things in detail with partners and family before implementing major decisions, rather than just making a choice and asking your partner to double-stamp it. This not only buys you time to work out a decision carefully, but also demonstrates to your teen that many issues involving them have consequences for others and that these must, therefore, be thought through, rather than simply given the go-ahead. By doing this, you are also modelling consultation and consideration in a relationship.

Once they hit puberty it's time to start preparing for the process of long-term separation, which is all too necessary. You have to separate so that they can grow up and run their own lives and make their own decisions. Like anyone, they will make good ones and not-so-good ones, but they will run their lives *their* way. You may feel sidelined, but don't lose sight of the fact that you are very important still, and if you let them go, in all probability they will come back to you to form a new adult relationship – this time one in which you are equals.

It's common for parents to feel both relieved and lost when their children first leave home or start living away for much of the year. However, it can be a time for doing all those things there were never time for before and for getting a whole new lease on life. Exploring interests and meeting new people can make it an exciting time with a bit of effort.

As we discussed at the very start of this book, parenting the B&C child is not easy but it can be enormously rewarding. Throughout this book we have tried to make the steps and strategies you need to adopt clear and easy to follow using examples from other parents and families to help you relate the issues to everyday child behaviour.

By now you will be aware of many of the ways in which your child matches the experiences of other parents and many of the ways in which they differ – each child is an individual.

The journey of parenting never stops, nor do the day-to-day trials and tribulations, but by using the strategies and techniques we have described in *It's Not Fair!* with patience and commitment, you will soon find that the many joys and delights increase and concerns decrease.

Good luck!

Resources

Supporting Children

ChildLine
Free, twenty-four-hour helpline for children and young people in danger or distress: 0800 1111
www.childline.org.uk

Get Connected
Provides young people with assistance finding a service to help them, whatever the problem.
Free helpline: 0800 808 4994
www.getconnected.org.uk

General Advice and Citizenship

Adviceguide
The online service from the Citizens Advice Bureau that gives you information on your rights in all countries of the UK (not always the same) and on a wide range of topics, including benefits and employment and debt and legal issues. Some content is in Welsh, and also ethnic community languages.
www.adviceguide.org.uk

Ask Jeeves Kids
Service to help children to search the Internet for answers to their varied questions.
www.askkids.com

Bereavement

Cruse
Offers nationwide bereavement support and information; their website is: www.crusebereavementcare.org.uk. They also offer a special support website for young people called rd4u – this is designed for the young by the young, and its main aim is to help you find your own road to dealing with your loss.
www.rd4u.org.uk email: info@rd4u.org.uk
Young persons' freephone helpline: 0808 808 1677

Bullying

An anti-bullying website for young people:
www.bbclic.com

Anti-bullying helpline for parents:
www.kidscape.org.uk

Help on all forms of bullying – at school, cyberbullying, racism, homophobia, bullying in sport, etc.:
www.bullying.co.uk

Drugs

Free confidential advice and information on drugs twenty-four hours a day:
www.talktofrank.com

Information and advice on drugs and the law:
www.release.org.uk

Family Break-up

NCH – It's Not Your Fault
Practical information for children, young people and parents going through a family break-up.
www.itsnotyourfault.org

Young Carers

Advice, support and information for children and young people who have a caring responsibility for someone in their family with a physical or mental illness, a disability or substance misuse problem. The site also contains a section with information for parents.
www.youngcarers.net

Fathers

Dads Space (Atticmedia and Respect)
A website offering no-nonsense advice and information based on dads' own experiences and up-to-date research.
www.dads-space.com

Dad Talk (Family Matters Institute)

A website for dads – champions fatherhood and explores what it is to be a dad in twenty-first-century Britain.
www.dadtalk.co.uk

Families Need Fathers

Information and support on shared parenting following separation or divorce.
www.fnf.org.uk

Separated Dads

Being separated from your kids can be hard if you're a dad. This website helps with ideas on how to cope when you are together or apart.
www.separateddads.co.uk

Education

The Advisory Centre for Education

The ASKACE Service recently won recognition from the BT/THA Helplines Award 2008 for innovative use of technology to deliver a helpline service.

How to get advice: text the keyword ASKACE to 68808 and follow the instructions for free booklets, tips and advice tailored to your questions.

General advice line (Monday–Friday, 10 a.m.–5 p.m.): 0808 800 5793

Exclusion information line (twenty-four-hour answerphone): 020 7704 9822

Exclusion advice line (Monday–Friday 10 a.m.–5 p.m.): 0808 800 0327

www.ace-ed.org.uk

BBC
www.bbc.co.uk/schools/parents/

Homework Elephant
Resources to help children complete their homework. www.homeworkelephant.co.uk

ParentsCentre
Information and help on supporting your children with learning and the education system.
www.parentscentre.gov.uk

Emotional Wellbeing

Family and Parenting Institute
Charity aiming to improve the wellbeing of children and families in the UK.
www.familyandparenting.org

Understanding Childhood
Provides free downloadable information leaflets for families and childcare professionals to help raise emotionally secure children.
www.understandingchildhood.net

Young Minds
Information for parents who may be concerned about the mental health of their child.
www.youngminds.org.uk

Networking

Netmums
A unique local network for mums (or dads) offering a wealth of information on both a national and local level. Once registered, you can access details for all kinds of local resources, from child-friendly cafés to childminders and places to go.
www.netmums.com

Parents' Advice Centre (Northern Ireland)
Provides a telephone helpline and face-to-face support and guidance for families on issues such as bullying, separation/divorce, self-harm and emotional difficulties.
www.parentsadvicecentre.org

Gingerbread
Free information to lone parents including benefits, tax and housing.
www.oneparentfamilies.org.uk

Gambling

Information, advice and practical help in relation to gambling.
www.gamcare.org.uk

Grandparents

The Grandparents' Association
The fastest growing membership organisation for grandparents in the country.
www.grandparents-association.org.uk

Health

Children First
A free general health information website for young people and families. Run by Great Ormond Street Hospital, it provides authoritative and clinically approved advice from child health experts on a broad range of health-related topics.
www.childrenfirst.nhs.uk

beat (formerly Eating Disorders Association)
Information and support across the UK.
www.b-eat.co.uk

NHS Direct
Information on health, illness and the NHS.
www.nhsdirect.nhs.uk

Internet Safety

Childnet International – Know IT All
Website with resources aimed at young people, parents and teachers about safe and positive use of the Internet. It contains information about what the risks are to users and outlines practical advice in avoiding or minimising risks when using online and mobile technologies.
www.childnet.com

Home Office
Leaflet on children using the Internet safely.
www.thinkuknow.co.uk

Internet Watch Foundation

Site for reporting potentially illegal online content, specifically child abuse images and content hosted anywhere in the world, criminally obscene content hosted in the UK and incitement to racial hatred content hosted in the UK.
www.iwf.org.uk

Kidsmart

Practical Internet safety programme website for schools, young people, parents and agencies, produced by the children's Internet charity Childnet International.
www.kidsmart.org.uk

Self-harm

A key information resource for young people who self-harm, their friends and family, and for the professionals who work with them:
www.selfharm.org.uk

Sex and Relationships

FPA

Provides publications and recommendations, useful signposting and training.
www.fpa.org.uk

Sex Education Forum

Aims to create an environment that keeps sex and relationship education (SRE) on the agenda and shares information among professionals and parents/carers, to support them with planning and delivering good-quality SRE.
www.ncb.org.uk

Index